Unleashed

Living a Fully Integrated Life

TABLE OF CONTENTS

TABLE OF CONTENTS

SMALL GROUP GUIDELINES

When beginning a group, or when new people join your group, review these guidelines for participating in a small group. These guidelines are intended to help create an environment where everyone feels safe to participate and share openly.

Safe Zone: Allow space for people to be heard and accepted.

Confidentiality: Whatever is shared during the group should not be shared outside of group with anyone unless it is your story, or you have received permission from the person who shared it.

Respect: When someone is giving their view or testimony, please do not interrupt. Allow them to complete their thought before asking questions or sharing your view.

Give your story, not advice: When someone shares do not respond with advice unless they specifically ask for it. If you begin a sentence with "you should" then it's advice.

Share your story: We all grow by hearing from each other. God brought you through your struggles to help someone else through theirs.

Allow time for others: We want to hear your story, but allow time for others to share as well.

HOW TO USE YOUR STUDY GUIDE

Each week, your group facilitator will take you through a series of scriptures related to a relevant work topic. Your study guide is divided into several sections to help facilitate your discussion.

Opening Discussion: We will begin each week with a question related to the topic for the week to help focus our attention and open the dialogue for all to participate.

Scripture: Take turns reading aloud our related scriptures for the week.

Group Discussion: Spend some time reviewing questions and discussing thoughts about the scripture.

Challenge for the Week: In order to allow the Holy Spirit to really make a lasting impact in our lives, we have to challenge ourselves to act on what we learn over the course of the week. Select a buddy from your group to help encourage one another and hold each other accountable.

Memory Verse: Each week we will have a key scripture to hold onto and memorize. Post this up in your office, on your bathroom mirror, on the refrigerator, or any other location you will see every day.

Closing Prayer: We will end in prayer, thanking God for his presence during the study and lifting up anyone in the group who is in need of prayer.

INTRODUCTION

I always thought I was a good Christian and a successful businesswoman. I was surprised when my manager pulled me into her office and said, "I know you go to church, serve at youth group and feed the homeless, but why are you a different person when you are here at work?" As it turns out, I was a good Christian and a successful businesswoman, but not at the same time. I thought faith and work were two very separate entities.

God was certainly not completely absent from my work. I would offer prayer for co-workers in times of need, and I led a women's Bible study for some of my co-workers and friends over lunch. However, the comment from my manager began to bring some questions to mind about my faith and work. Could it be possible that God wanted to be part of my WHOLE life and not just the super spiritual spaces I would set apart for Him? Was there a greater purpose for my work?

Over the next few years, I became aware that God wanted me to learn to trust Him and relinquish control of my life plan. As my trust grew, my faith did as well. This growth process ultimately led to the biggest risk and leap of faith in my life, letting go of a driven and successful 22-year career in Corporate America. I clearly heard the Lord tell me it was time to go, be still, surrender control to Him, and trust He would show me what to do next. On November 18th, 2016, I left an executive level job without a plan, no new career path and no one to support me financially.

While I didn't fully understand what that meant at the time, I believed there was going to be something great on the other end of my decision. This was the space I needed. Space to sit with God, to get to know Him as Father and understand His love for me. Space for rest, healing, and ultimately to prepare for what was to come.

Within days of the announcement that I was leaving, countless women approached me to set up time to talk. They were struggling with the intense over-reaching demands in the workplace and felt unsafe telling anyone. Trying to succeed according to the world's standards meant compromising time with family, friends and self-care. Some shared stories of wanting to quit, but being too afraid to do it. My heart was breaking for the amount of pain and isolation they were experiencing on a daily basis, but hiding it— just like I had. No one knew about my stress and anxiety attacks. Listening to these women I had worked alongside for years, and realizing we were all struggling in silence and isolation, it began to feel like God had pulled me out so I could see more clearly how to help minister back into the place I just left. To be perfectly honest, I didn't want to accept this calling. While I had grown up in the church, I had never participated in women's ministry. I had never felt like I belonged in those groups because I was single, worked and didn't have kids. I was also concerned with how I would make money to support myself, and didn't see starting a non-profit as the best way to do that. Fear and uncertainty were certainly trying to keep me from moving forward. I was feeling not Christian enough, not smart enough, unqualified and ill-equipped. Certainly, this was not the path God intended for me! I was really, really good at my job: achieving sales and profit, succeeding in negotiations, creating new product concepts, etc. This new path was completely unfamiliar.

In January 2017, believing I was being led to help these women, I asked a few friends to get together to see if they would like to be part of a small group study. We ended up with three groups and decided to study Rick Warren's *A Purpose Driven Life*. Everyone liked it, but still struggled with understanding how to integrate their faith in the workplace. I remember thinking, "I don't know either, that's one of the reasons I quit my job!" I researched for curriculum on-line and asked others, but none could be found. I went to God and asked him for direction on what to do and heard Him say, "You write it." I quickly responded with "I can't. I'm not a writer, I don't know the Bible well enough and certainly was never successful with living out my faith in the workplace." Then He replied, "You can do all things through me." At this point I conceded, and responded, "Yes. Ok. I understand, but you are going to have to show me how to do this."

Every single step was unknown and felt impossible. Not knowing how anything would turn out before taking a step forward left me in full dependence on God. Since I believed He was the one providing direction, moving forward in obedience was the only appropriate response. My confidence shifted from my own ability to accomplish the task to God's ability to equip me. He brought the following scripture:

"May He equip you with all you need for doing his will. May He produce in you, through the power of Jesus Christ, every good thing that is pleasing to Him. All glory to Him forever and ever! Amen." -Hebrews 13:21(NLT)

Little did I know how foundational this scripture would become in my life. Within a couple of weeks, He introduced me to three writers who would help make His vision for a ministry called *Women in the Marketplace* a reality. I met a blogger, a writing mentor and a third writer who provided an outline for our curriculum. This would be the exact framework we needed to get started. Our current groups spent some time brainstorming topics, and then I went away with outline in hand to try to put together our first study. I had no idea what I was doing or how this was going to work, but God had a plan.

Women in the Marketplace was created to help women discover how to integrate their faith into the workplace. The small groups are a space to gather in order to grow in faith and build relationships that provide strength and encouragement along the way. Our study guides were initially topic focused and combined scripture with everyday work situations to help provide direction, challenge thinking and spark empowering conversation. As we have evolved in our ministry, we are now providing one workbook to help unleash the power of the Holy Spirit in your life.

Our *Unleashed* journey begins with our minds and the choice we have to make to allow the Holy Spirit into ALL of our work, not just the moments of prayer or a bible study. When we allow our faith and relationship with God to be evident in all we do, we find incredible power and true purpose for our work.

The second section is the outward release of the Holy Spirit into the relationships around us. This is a deep dive into Romans 12 and what that means to love each other in the workplace and why it is so important to our God.

The third section pulls everything together for walking out God's plan for the good life. This final section helps provide the framework for living a fully integrated life, where any constraint we might have is removed to allow the Spirit to flow freely. As this happens, the fruits of the Spirits are released in our lives and out to those around us.

We are excited to have you on this journey with us. We hope that you will find surprising relationships built with others and enrichment in your relationship with God. We pray you will want to spread the word to others who are stuck in believing work is toil, only a way to make a living, not a place where your faith is active. It is our hope that you will truly discover the good life and eagerly lead others to do the same.

Kathy Book
Founder, *Women in the Marketplace*
www.womeninmarketplace.net

Unleashed

Section 1

Releasing Power and Purpose in Your Work

POWER & PURPOSE

SESSION 1

INTRODUCTION

Opening Discussion:

Often times, we compartmentalize our lives between work, home, family, friends, etc. We might take on different roles in each of these environments depending on our personal responsibilities, expectations or social norms. We might believe this is a healthy approach because it creates boundaries or work-life balance. However, there is one aspect of our lives that is not intended to be limited to a single space, and that is our faith. The Holy Spirit is inside of us. It is with us every place we go, not just at church on Sunday. When we keep our faith separate from our work-life, we put limits on what is possible in our work and diminish the purpose we can find in it.

Is your relationship with God confined to morning devotion or church? How open are you to inviting Him into your daily work? What would it look like to do this?

____

____

Do you think integrating your faith into your work would bring you an advantage or disadvantage? What are some examples of both?

____

____

One of the incredible advantages of integrating your faith and work life is the unleashing of the power within us to transform our every thought, feeling and action. Over the course of this study, we are going to work together to allow God to transform the way we think about our work. As we change the way we think, it will change how we feel. When our feelings change, our attitude shifts and our behavior begins to align with the Spirit within us. This opens up space for God's Kingdom to come, and His will to be done here, as in heaven.

As we begin, let's consider what it means for something to be unleashed. If you have ever had a dog, you have probably used a leash. There is a snap hook on the end of a line that connects to a ring on the collar of the dog. To unleash it, you have to open up the hook and release the collar. Similarly, for us to unleash the power and purpose of God in our work, we have to open ourselves as well.

What might a posture of openness look like for us? What do you need to release?

____

____

David demonstrated his spiritual openness by physically stretching out His hands to God, submitting that he needed Him the way dry land needs water.

I stretch out my hands to you; my soul thirsts for you like a parched land.
Psalm 143:6

With this same posture, our hands open to receive, let's listen to Paul's prayer to the Ephesians:

*I pray that your hearts will be flooded with light so that you can **understand the confident hope** he has given to those he called—his holy people who are his rich and glorious inheritance. I also pray that you will **understand the incredible greatness of God's power** for us who believe him.*
Ephesians 1:18-19

Group Discussion:
Paul prays for hearts to be "flooded with light so that" what can happen?

____

____

Notice he doesn't pray they receive confident hope and incredible power. Why? Because they already possess it. Instead he prays for light to illuminate their hearts so they understand what is already there. We typically think of understanding as something that comes from our mind. It is important to note Paul is praying for understanding in our heart. This is a deeper level of understanding from which we can fully utilize the incredible power inside.

Until you understand the incredible power you bring, it will lie dormant inside, just waiting for you to release it.

Challenge for the week:
This week's challenge is to spend some time thinking about the space you create in your work day for God to be present. Are you open to inviting God to join you in your work?

____

____

Spend some quiet time with God asking Him to help you understand the greatness you bring into your day and how you might unleash it.

Create a reminder that will prompt you during your day to acknowledge He is with you.

Prayer Requests:

POWER & PURPOSE

SESSION 2

THE CHOICE

Opening Discussion:
During session one, we discussed the importance of understanding the incredible power we have inside as believers. We challenged each other to consider how we might become more aware of it during our workday.

How have you found ways to create space for God in your work? If you haven't, what do you think has held you back?

____

____

Here is the interesting thing about having this incredible power in our lives: even when we begin to understand it, we have to choose to unleash it. Today we are going to explore this choice, and how saying "yes" unleashes God's power in our lives.

> *¹ One day as Jesus was standing by the Lake of Gennesaret, the people were crowding around him and listening to the word of God. ² He saw at the water's edge two boats, left there by the fishermen, who were washing their nets. ³ He got into one of the boats, the one belonging to Simon, and asked him to put out a little from shore. Then he sat down and taught the people from the boat.*
>
> *⁴ When he had finished speaking, he said to Simon, "Put out into deep water, and let down the nets for a catch."*
>
> *⁵ Simon answered, "Master, we've worked hard all night and haven't caught anything. But because you say so, I will let down the nets."*
>
> *⁶ When they had done so, they caught such a large number of fish that their nets began to break. ⁷ So they signaled their partners in the other boat to come and help them, and they came and filled both boats so full that they began to sink.*
>
> Luke 5:1-7

Group Discussion:
Simon and the disciples witnessed a miracle. They saw the power of Jesus unleashed in their work. They were fisherman trying to catch fish. When Jesus said to put the nets back out,

Simon questioned him because of their lack of success all night. Yet through his choice to obey, the power of Jesus was unleashed, and they caught more than the boat could hold.

Do you believe God cares about the success of your work? Why or why not?

____

____

Jesus asked Simon to put the net out in deep water, something different from the way he thought it should be done. Simon's job was knowing how to catch fish, yet he submitted to Jesus in obedience. When you feel like the Holy Spirit is prompting you to do something, how do you respond? Do you question it based on your own wisdom? Obey quickly? Delay obedience? Dismiss it altogether? Share an example with your group.

____

____

Even after we witness the incredible greatness of God's power, we don't always decide to invite Him into our work-life. What are some reasons why we might not make this choice?

____

____

After witnessing the power of Jesus in his work, wouldn't you think Simon would want to take Him along on every expedition? Let's turn back to the Book of Luke and see how he responded:

> [8] *When Simon Peter saw this, he fell at Jesus' knees and said, "Go away from me, Lord; I am a sinful man!"* [9] *For he and all his companions were astonished at the catch of fish they had taken,* [10] *and so were James and John, the sons of Zebedee, Simon's partners.*
>
> *Then Jesus said to Simon, "Don't be afraid; from now on you will fish for people."* [11] *So they pulled their boats up on shore, left everything and followed him.*
>
> Luke 5:8-11

Group Discussion:
What are your thoughts about Simon Peter's response to witnessing the power of Jesus in his work? How can you relate to how he felt?

____

____

Jesus responds with "don't be afraid." Could it be fear that is holding you back from inviting God into your work? Are you ever afraid of what God might ask you to do if you open your work to Him?

____

____

If we can learn to trust that God wants a fulfilling life for us, what He dreamt for us before we were born, then perhaps we can begin to release our control over to Him, unleashing confident hope and incredible power in our work. The choice is yours.

Challenge for the week:
This week's challenge is to look for ways to invite God into your work. Choose to say yes to any prompting you have from the Holy Spirit to act. Write about your experience below.

____

____

Prayer Requests:

POWER & PURPOSE

SESSION 3

KINGDOM PERSPECTIVE

Opening Discussion:
We talked in session one about creating space to allow our minds to center on God's presence within our work. Last session we saw from Peter's example that miracles can happen when we obey in spite of what we think we know from experience. Unleashing the power of God in our work, enables us to think about people, process and success differently than the way the world sees them. Throughout our time together, we are going to call this looking at our work from a Kingdom perspective.

Kingdom perspective requires us to shift our thinking, thought patterns and what is filling our minds from the world's viewpoint to God's viewpoint. It can be extremely difficult because we are surrounded by the allure of personal and financial success, titles and independence. This is the vantage point from which most people think and make decisions about their lives.

How do you think about your work, the company and your co-workers? Are you generally able to maintain a positive attitude throughout the day? If not, why?

____

____

When something goes wrong, do you typically focus on the positive or negative of the situation? Why do you think you respond one way or the other?

____

____

How we feel about our day is often determined by what happens around us, whether good or bad. If we unleash the power of the Holy Spirit into our work, we can learn to transform our thoughts in order to maintain a better overall mindset throughout our day.

> *Do not be conformed to this world, but be transformed by the **renewal of your mind**, that by testing you may discern what is the will of God, what is good and acceptable and perfect.*
>
> Romans 12:2

> *You were taught, with regard to your former way of life, to put off your old self, which is being corrupted by its deceitful desires; to be **made new in the attitude of your minds**; and to put on the new self, created to be like God in true righteousness and holiness.*
>
> Ephesians 4:22-24

Group Discussion:
How do we renew our minds or be made new in the attitude of our minds?

____

____

One way we can renew the attitude of our minds is to replace our thoughts with The Kingdom perspective or how God would view the situation.

> And now, dear brothers and sisters, one final thing. **Fix your thoughts** on what is **true**, and **honorable**, and **right**, and **pure**, and **lovely**, and **admirable**. Think about things that are **excellent** and **worthy of praise**. Keep putting into practice all you learned and received from me— everything you heard from me and saw me doing. Then the God of peace will be with you.
>
> Philippians 4:8–9

Fix your thoughts...did you catch that? Most versions of the Bible say "think about these things."

This version of scripture speaks to the emphasis on "fix." It is a much stronger word than just thinking about something. Fixing your thoughts has an unwavering action to it. It not only securely holds God's truth in our minds, but it mends or repairs the worldly or negative thoughts that try and take up space there.

If we set our minds on bringing God's will into the moments of our lives, we will begin to see situations from His viewpoint, or a Kingdom perspective. When our thoughts do not line up, we can learn to take them captive and fix them.

> We demolish arguments and every pretension that sets itself up against the knowledge of God, and we **take captive every thought** to make it obedient to Christ.
>
> 2 Corinthians 10:5

Group discussion:
Share a time when you have had to take a thought captive and transform it. How did you do it?

____

____

Personal Exercise:
Paul says if we put this into practice, we will have peace. Let's give it a try right now. Think about a situation that happened this week that upset you.

____

____

Once you have the thought, go through these steps:

1. Review your experience in light of our scripture. Place a "✓" next to each one that aligns with your thought:

    - ☐ It is **true**.
    - ☐ It **honors** the other person.
    - ☐ It is **right** and just.
    - ☐ My motivation is **pure.**
    - ☐ It is **lovely.**
    - ☐ It is **admirable.**
    - ☐ Is it **excellent.**
    - ☐ It is **worthy of praise.** You would be proud to share it.

2. If your thought does not make it through the filter, then take it captive and fix it.

3. What is something positive about the person or situation? What good can come from it? Can you look at it from a different perspective and understand it better? What about it or the person is excellent and worthy of praise?

____

____

4. Think about those things.

Based on this exercise, how would a renewed mind offer an advantage to you in your work?

____

____

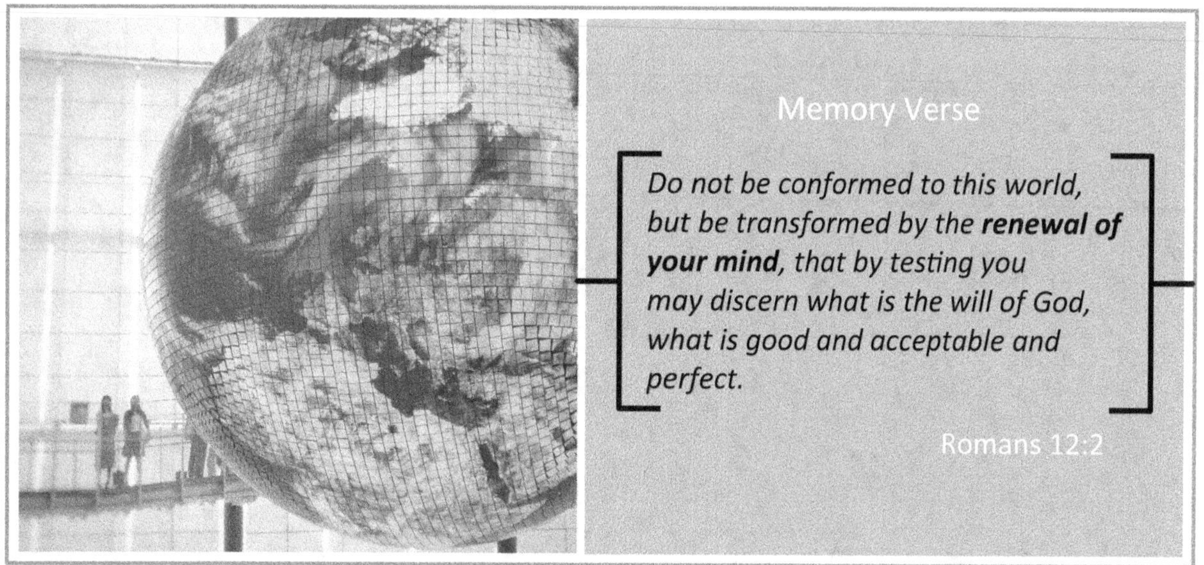

Challenge for the week:

This week's challenge is to begin to be aware of your thoughts in the moments of your day. Be mindful of the perspective from which you are thinking. When you find yourself thinking things that don't line up with God's heart or the Kingdom perspective, consider how you would change your thoughts so they line up. Use your checklist to guide you until it becomes a habit.

Prayer Requests:

POWER & PURPOSE

SESSION 4

PURPOSE FOR WORK

Opening Discussion:
We have been discussing practicing mindfulness throughout our day to help us transform our thoughts about situations that arise, but what is your overall attitude about work? Is it something you have to do in order to provide for yourself and your family? Does it feel like meaningless toil? Or is it life-giving?

> *For a person may labor with wisdom, knowledge and skill, and then they must leave all they own to another who has not toiled for it. This too is meaningless and a great misfortune. What do people get for all the toil and anxious striving with which they labor under the sun? All their days their work is grief and pain; even at night their minds do not rest. This too is meaningless.*
>
> Ecclesiastes 2:21-23

How do you feel about your work? Do you agree with King Solomon's assessment? Or does it bring you satisfaction, fulfillment and purpose?

____

____

Interestingly, no matter how we feel about our current job, we would likely still work, no matter how financially secure we were, because we were created to work.

Working was part of our design BEFORE the fall. Original sin entered into the world and work then became toil. However, because of Jesus, we have not only been restored with God for eternity, but also for the here and now.

Our work was included in this restoration.

If this is true, what does it mean for us today? How do we access the fullness of how work was designed to be for us? What is the purpose of it?

> *The LORD God took the man and put him in the Garden of Eden to* **work** *(avodah) it and take care of it.*
>
> Genesis 2:15

The Hebrew word "avodah" used here means work, worship, and service.

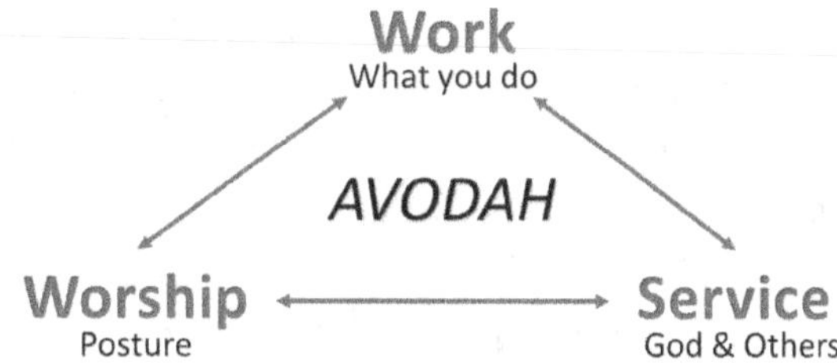

The world's view of work is singularly focused on **what** you do for a living. It is your position, title and how you make money. It's no wonder it feels like meaningless toil or a curse that produces thorns and thistles. The Kingdom perspective on work is so much more. God's view of our work combines what we do with worship and service. Think of this as a three-legged stool. If you try and sit on a stool with only one leg, it is extremely difficult to balance. Even if we have two of the legs, it is still hard to maintain balance. But a stool with all three legs working together, creates balance and a sturdy foundation. The unity of work, worship and service unleashes purpose in our work-life.

Group Discussion:
How would your view of work change if you looked at it in light of this concept? Is this possible?

____

____

Does it matter what career we choose? In other words is **_what_** we do for our job important? Why or why not?

____

____

What we do should never define who we are. However, the work we do is certainly a reflection of how we were designed and who created us.

> *There are different kinds of working, but in all of them and in everyone it is the same God at work.*
>
> 1 Corinthians 12:6

The position we hold might be very different, but what we have in common is that each of us is designed with certain gifts, strengths and abilities that are a direct reflection of our creator. Did you know that you were given specific strengths and abilities to help you do work while you are here? You might think something that just comes natural to you is something everyone can do. However, that often is not the case. It is likely a gift that was given to you for a specific assignment for the Kingdom.

*For we are his workmanship, created in Christ Jesus for **good works**, which God prepared beforehand, that we should walk in them.*
Ephesians 2:10

*For as in one body we have many members, and the members do not all have the same function, so we, though many, are one body in Christ, and individually members one of another. Having **gifts that differ** according to the grace given to us, let us use them: if prophecy, in proportion to our faith; if service, in our serving; the one who teaches, in his teaching; the one who exhorts, in his exhortation; the one who contributes, in generosity; the one who leads, with zeal; the one who does acts of mercy, with cheerfulness.*
Romans 12:4-8

Group Discussion:
How do these scripture help us understand the importance of what we do for our work?

____

____

Take a moment and share some of the gifts/talents you have. How are they contributing to your work? Are any of them not being exercised?

____

____

What we do is important because it is how we utilize the gifts and talents we have been given. It doesn't have to be a direct aspect of our paying job, but it is part of our life's work (purpose) while we are here on Earth.

Challenge for the week:
Perhaps you are not sure what talents you have been given. Spend some time this week in discovery.

1. Ask some friends and co-workers what strengths they see in you.

____

____

2. Take the FREE personal strengths assessment @ www.high5test.com. Capture your results here:

____

____

____

____

____

Set aside 15-20 minutes to talk with God about how your strengths line up with what you do. Ask Him to show your other ways you can utilize your strengths to build the Kingdom.

Be prepared to share one of your top 5 with your group next session.

Prayer Requests:

POWER & PURPOSE

SESSION 5

WORK IS WORSHIP

Opening Discussion:
What is one of your top 5 strengths from the assessment? How is it utilized in what you do currently?

____

____

If you recall from our last session, Avodah, God's view of work, is the unity of work, worship and service. What we do is not the singular purpose for work. Our work is also intended to be worship.

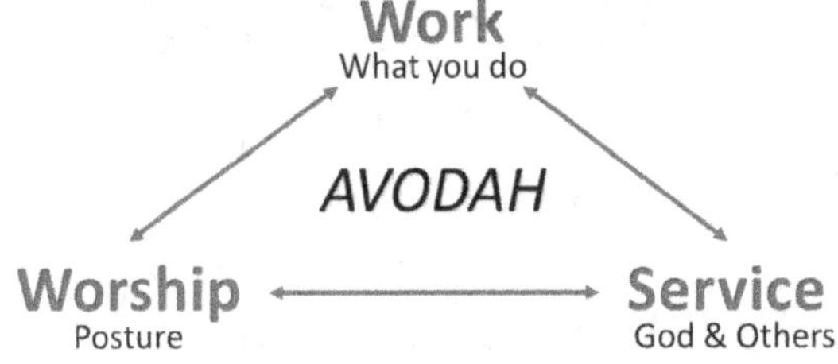

What is worship? Why do we do it? How do you express it?

____

____

> Therefore let us be **grateful for receiving a kingdom that cannot be shaken**, and thus let us offer to God acceptable **worship**, with reverence and awe, for our God is a consuming fire.
>
> Hebrews 12:28-29

Group Discussion:
How does this translate to your work? How can everything you do be an act of worship?

____

____

Everything we do can be an act of worship if our posture is towards God. Today we are going to discuss three simple ways we can incorporate worship into our daily work.

> ***Rejoice** always, **pray** continually, **give thanks** in all circumstances; for this is God's will for you in Christ Jesus.*
>
> 1 Thessalonians 5:16-18

REJOICE ALWAYS

Rejoicing is more of an attitude than an action. It flows from the choice of where you focus your thoughts. When you wake in the morning, you can be full of joy that God woke you for another day, so there is purpose in it. When you are walking through your day, you can be full of joy that God is walking with you and will never leave you. Finally, you can be full of joy at the end of the day as you think about the positive moments and goodness of your day.

> ***Always be full of joy** in the Lord. I say it again—rejoice!*
>
> Philippians 4:4

How can you incorporate an attitude of **rejoicing** in your day, especially at work?

____

____

PRAY CONTINUALLY

> *I urge you, first of all, to **pray for all people.** Ask God to help them; intercede on their behalf, and give thanks for them.*
>
> 1 Timothy 2:1 NLT

> *Don't worry about anything; instead, **pray about everything**. Tell God what you need, and thank him for all he has done.*
>
> Philippians 4:6

How do you pray for people at work? Why is it important to pray for ALL people? Do you pray for your leadership? How about the people who are difficult to work with? What is your prayer for them?

____

____

Our second scripture says to pray about EVERYTHING. Do you do this? Do you pray about the details of your job? How do you pray for situations and circumstances at your work? Share an example of something you prayed for in your work and how God answered you.

____

____

GIVE THANKS

*I will **give thanks** to you, LORD, with all my heart; I will tell of all your wonderful deeds.*

Psalm 9:1

As we start to work from a posture of worship, where our attitude is one of joy and our mind is set on prayer, our hearts will experience thankfulness in all circumstances. Thanksgiving is not intended to be kept quiet. When God answers our prayers, we share the wonderful news with others to give Him the glory.

Share an example of something God has done in your work, so we can all give thanks and praise Him in this moment.

____

____

How do we give thanks in all circumstances? Have you ever experienced what seemed to be something unsettling at work that later you were able to thank God for His plan?

____

____

Just as praise and worship are lifted up both in good times and when life hits us hard, so it is with our work. We rejoice, pray and give thanks to God for our work both when it is going well and when we are struggling and unsure of what tomorrow holds. Letting go of the worry and fear creates space for God to bring hope into all situations and move on our behalf.

Work as worship is about understanding that every task we do during our workday is intended to be done for God and with God.

Unleashing His power into our work, enables us to change the way we think about even the smallest, most dreaded task during our week. It takes on significant meaning and purpose because it is a loving, honoring response of thanksgiving and praise to our God.

Challenge for the week:
Spend some time each morning this week reviewing your calendar before you start your day.

Which meetings or tasks do you need to shift your thinking from work to worship?

____

____

____

How can you incorporate rejoicing, praying and giving thanks into your day?

____

____

____

Prayer Requests:

POWER & PURPOSE

SESSION 6

SERVE GOD

Opening Discussion:
Over the last few sessions, we have been talking about how our work is so much more than what we do. How it can also be an act of worship when we offer it in response to God through rejoicing, praying and giving thanks. The work we do has been prepared in advance for us and flows from our worship by using the gifts we have been given.

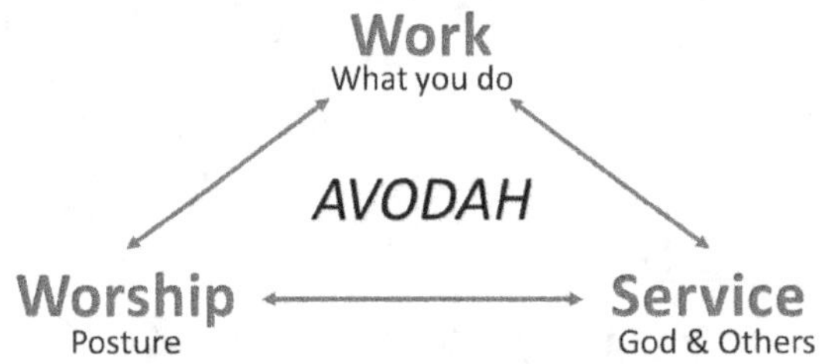

What about service? Who do you serve in your work?

____

____

Everything we do serves someone. Unfortunately, that can be ourselves if we are not living a fully integrated life.

> *No one can serve two masters. Either you will hate the one and love the other, or you will be devoted to the one and despise the other. You cannot serve both God and money.*
>
> Matthew 6:24

While our work is a means for us to make money, it should not be the purpose for our work. From the Kingdom perspective, it serves a greater purpose. It is intended to be service to God and others.

Serve God. Serve others.
Over the next two sessions, we are going to unpack what it looks like to serve God and others through our work. Today we are going to focus on how our work is service to God.

Group Discussion:
Does serving God feel like a duty or way to show your love for Him? What do you do to serve Him?

____

____

Have you ever considered your work as service to God? How can we serve God through our work?

____

____

We don't have to be a missionary or work at a church or non-profit to serve God in our work. There is an attitude with which we can work that will show others who you are serving. How you do your work is as important as what you do.

> *Never be lazy, but **work hard** and serve the Lord **enthusiastically**.*
> Romans 12:11 (NLT)

> *Do all things **without grumbling or disputing**; so that you will prove yourselves to be blameless and innocent, children of God above reproach in the midst of a crooked and perverse generation, among whom you **appear as lights in the world**, holding fast the word of life, so that in the day of Christ I will have reason to glory because I did not run in vain nor toil in vain.*
> Philippians 2:14-16

Work is not toil when our heart is set on serving God. It becomes an opportunity to show our love for Him and be a light in the world.

Group Discussion:
Do you believe how you approach your work could actually show people your faith and love for God? How is that possible?

____

____

Let's recap a few ways Paul suggests we might serve God through our work:

- ♦ Work hard (Romans 12:11) — *give yourself fully, be engaged and focused*
- ♦ Work with enthusiasm (Romans 12:11) — *be joyful*
- ♦ Without grumbling or disputing (Philippians 2:14) — *keep a positive attitude*
- ♦ Appear as lights in the world (Philippians 2:15) — *be a light in your workplace*

Which of these is an area of strength for you? Which one might be an area that needs improvement?

____

____

What would it take for you to put these ideas into practice?

____

____

We can serve God through mission work, helping the homeless or other philanthropic ways, but if we shut Him out of our work, we are missing a significant part of our daily lives. He created us to work. Why not glorify Him by serving Him daily through how we go about our work? Your work pleases God. Let it be a reflection of your faith.

Challenge for the week:
Review the ways your work can be service to God. Look at the tasks you do this week as an opportunity to display your faith and your love for God.

Prayer Requests:

POWER & PURPOSE

SESSION 7

SERVE OTHERS

Opening Discussion:

Last session we talked about our work being an opportunity to serve God and show our love for Him. When we serve God our work is worship, the same love God has for us overflows, spilling out to those around us.

Work is an opportunity to express God's love to others through serving them.

Practically every type of work involves some interaction with others. Even if we work alone, we have to sell our product or service to others. These interactions provide an opportunity for us to express God's love. Again, it doesn't matter what role or position you have. God has given all of us the same authority and responsibility as it relates to sharing His love. It's how people will know that we are His disciples.

> *"I give you a new command: Love one another. Just as I have loved you,*
> *you must also love one another. By this all people will know that you are*
> *My disciples, if you have love for one another."*
>
> John 13:34-35

Every encounter with someone at work is an opportunity to express God's love for that person by serving them. We can do this by putting other's interests above our own:

> *Therefore if you have any encouragement from being united with Christ, if*
> *any comfort from his love, if any common sharing in the Spirit, if any*
> *tenderness and compassion, then make my joy complete by being like-*
> *minded, **having the same love**, being one in spirit and of one mind. Do*
> *nothing out of selfish ambition or vain conceit. Rather, in humility value*
> *others above yourselves, not looking to your own interests but each of*
> *you to the interests of the others.*
>
> Philippians 2:1-4

We serve others through our work by allowing the same spirit we have offered to God in our worship to be unleashed to all those around us. We can demonstrate God's love in our relationships, through showing compassion, love and respect for each person we encounter.

Where there is compassion, there is passion to serve.

In everything I did, I showed you that by this kind of hard work we must **help the weak**, *remembering the words the Lord Jesus himself said: "It is more blessed to give than to receive."*

Acts 20:35

Group discussion:
What breaks your heart? Those are the areas where you will feel the most purpose in serving. Who are you helping?

____

____

LOVE

Love excludes no one.

If someone says, "I love God," but hates a fellow believer, that person is a liar; for if we don't love people we can see, how can we love God, whom we cannot see? And he has given us this command: Those who love God must also love their fellow believers.

1 John 4:20-21

What does it mean to love our co-workers? How do we do it? We can find some great advice in an unexpected scripture that we so often hear at weddings. Think about your co-workers as you listen.

Love is patient, love is kind. It does not envy, it does not boast, it is not proud. It does not dishonor others, it is not self-seeking, it is not easily angered, it keeps no record of wrongs. Love does not delight in evil but rejoices with the truth. It always protects, always trusts, always hopes, always perseveres.

1 Corinthians 13:4-7

Group Discussion:
How well do you love those around you at work? What are some ways this scripture helps us show our love for others?

____

____

What part of the scripture do you find difficult to do at work?

____

____

RESPECT

Honor leadership.

> *Dear brothers and sisters, **honor** those who are your leaders in the Lord's work. They work hard among you and give you spiritual guidance. Show them great **respect** and wholehearted love because of their work. And live peacefully with each other.*
>
> 1 Thessalonians 5:12-13

Group Discussion:
How do you show respect for leadership when you disagree with their decision or have conflicting personalities or moral standards?

____

____

What you do for work may or may not line up ideally with your gifts and talents, but it always creates a space for you to worship God and serve Him. It also provides opportunities to love and serve others. As you continue to find ways to unify work, worship and service, you will release your unique Kingdom purpose into your work.

Challenge for the week:
Show God's love through your actions. Be intentional. Do one thing this week for someone, while at work, to let that person know that God loves them.

Prayer Requests:

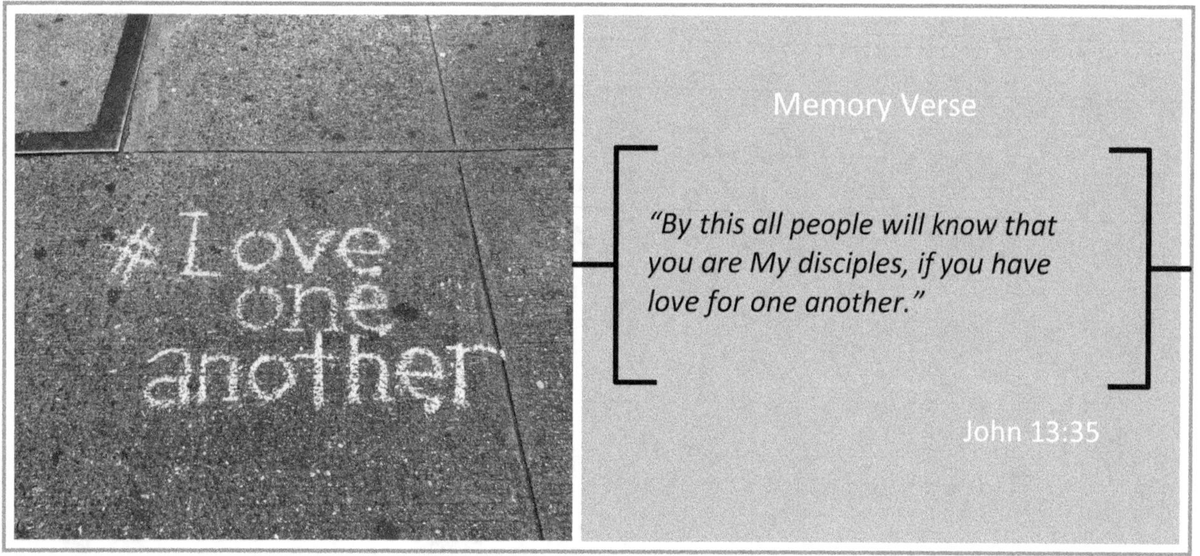
#Love
one
another

Memory Verse

"By this all people will know that
you are My disciples, if you have
love for one another."

John 13:35

POWER & PURPOSE

SESSION 8

SETTING OUR AIM

Opening Discussion:
Take a minute and think about what the word "success" means to you? What are some thoughts that come to mind?

____

____

Webster defines success as "the attainment of popularity or profit" or "a person or thing that achieves desired aims or attained prosperity."

What is your desired aim for your work? Why do you want to be successful?

____

____

In a dream the Lord told Solomon to ask for anything, and He would give it to him.

Here is what the young king asked:

> *"Now, Lord my God, you have made your servant king in place of my father David. But I am only a little child and do not know how to carry out my duties. Your servant is here among the people you have chosen, a great people, too numerous to count or number. So give your servant a discerning heart to govern your people and to distinguish between right and wrong. For who is able to govern this great people of yours?"*
>
> 1 Kings 3:7-9

Group Discussion:
What do you think King Solomon's desired aim for success was based on this scripture?

____

____

We find a humble, uncertain young king seeking wisdom and discernment in order to better serve God's people. Sounds a lot like our discussion the last few sessions about serving God and serving others. God was pleased with his selfless request, so He gave Solomon what he asked plus wealth and honor.

King Solomon reigned for 40 years. With his servant leader mindset and outward focused start, we might all agree he had set the right aim for success.

Let's take a look at the end of his reign to see how it went:

> *I undertook great projects: I built houses for myself and planted vineyards. I made gardens and parks and planted all kinds of fruit trees in them. I made reservoirs to water groves of flourishing trees. I bought male and female slaves and had other slaves who were born in my house. I also owned more herds and flocks than anyone in Jerusalem before me. I amassed silver and gold for myself, and the treasure of kings and provinces. I acquired male and female singers, and a harem as well—the delights of a man's heart. I became greater by far than anyone in Jerusalem before me. In all this my wisdom stayed with me.*
> *I denied myself nothing my eyes desired;*
> *I refused my heart no pleasure.*
> *My heart took delight in all my labor,*
> *and this was the reward for all my toil.*

Ecclesiastes 2:4-10

Group Discussion:
Review the scripture above. Underline or circle every time Solomon refers to himself. How many instances did you find?

____

____

How does this differ from the young King Solomon we discussed earlier? What do you think caused this significant shift in focus from others to self?

____

____

Power, popularity, prosperity, wealth, women and wisdom, King Solomon was a living definition of worldly success, but did he achieve his desired aim for success we discussed earlier?

Here is how he summed up his life achievement:

> *Yet when I surveyed all that my hands had done*
> *and what I had toiled to achieve,*
> *everything was meaningless, a chasing after the wind;*
> *nothing was gained under the sun.*
>
> Ecclesiastes 2:4-11

Group Discussion:
How have you related to Solomon's story? When do you find yourself struggling to stay focused on the Kingdom perspective of success?

____

____

Sometimes we, like Solomon, get caught up in worldly desires for success and forget we are part of a bigger story. You were given talents, but they aren't for your personal gain. Remember the money in the parable of the talents? That was the master's money which he entrusted to the servants while he was away. Our bigger story is that our Father has entrusted us with certain gifts and abilities that will bring His Kingdom to earth. We can choose to use them to build for Him or our own gain.

> *Do you not know that in a race all the runners run, but only one gets the*
> *prize? Run in such a way as to get the prize. Everyone who competes in*
> *the games goes into strict training. They do it to get a crown that will not*
> *last, but we do it to get a crown that will last forever.*
>
> 1 Corinthians 9:24-25

Where are you going to set your aim? Will it be on earthly treasure and the world's view of success? Or on a crown that will last forever?

Challenge for the week:
Spend some quiet time with God reflecting on your view of success. Consider journaling what lasting success looks like in your work. Where are you currently missing the mark and how might you redirect your aim?

Prayer Requests:

Memory Verse

Do you not know that in a race all the runners run, but only one gets the prize? Run in such a way as to get the prize.

1 Corinthians 9:24

POWER & PURPOSE

SESSION 9

LASTING SUCCESS

Opening Discussion:
We ended our last session talking about setting our aim on a crown that lasts forever. What does that mean? What are some things that last forever?

____

____

If you recall King Solomon from our last discussion, he realized that although he had gained every possession under the sun, none of it mattered for none of it could be kept or enjoyed after he passed from this life. The work to gain it didn't count for anything upon leaving this world. He wrote:

> *Everyone comes naked from their mother's womb, and as everyone*
> *comes, so they depart. They take nothing from their toil that they can*
> *carry in their hands. This too is a grievous evil: As everyone comes, so they*
> *depart, and what do they gain, since they toil for the wind?*
>
> Ecclesiastes 5:15-16

Group Discussion:
The house, car, money, job, none of it can be taken with you. If this is true, what is the purpose of generating wealth while we are here?

____

____

A hint is found in the Book of Luke when Jesus tells the story of the dishonest manager. In the story, a manager was fired by the owner of a business. The fired manager went out and re-wrote the debts people owed the owner so the debt on the ledger approximately 50% of the true debt. He was using money to gain friends, so when he lost his job, there would be someone there for him. The business owner actually applauded the ex-manager for his shrewdness. Jesus used this story to teach a lesson about wealth:

> *Here's the lesson: Use your worldly resources to benefit others and make*
> *friends. Then, when your possessions are gone, they will welcome you to*
> *an eternal home.*
>
> Luke 16:9

Group Discussion:
Is Jesus suggesting we use worldly wealth to make friends? What are your thoughts on this?

____

____

> *Teach those who are rich in this world not to be proud and not to trust in their money, which is so unreliable. Their trust should be in God, who richly gives us all we need for our enjoyment. Tell them to use their money to do good. They should be rich in good works and generous to those in need, always being ready to share with others. By doing this they will be storing up their treasure as a good foundation for the future so that they may experience **true life**.*
>
> 1 Timothy 6:17-19 NLT

What is the treasure that Paul suggests we are storing up by helping others? Could it be the same thing Jesus is describing in Luke 16?

____

____

It is important to note that none of these scriptures say that worldly wealth is bad. Actually, the more prosperous you are, the more you can help others. The caution against worldly wealth is to not rely on it as our source of security, happiness or become prideful in what you have. If our focus becomes solely on the money or earthly things, we will miss out on the joy they can bring us. Jesus spoke about this idea as well:

> *And he went on to say to them all, "Watch out and guard yourselves from every kind of greed; because your **true life** is not made up of the things you own, no matter how rich you may be."*
>
> Luke 12:15 ESV

"True life is not made up of things you own," and success is not defined by your title, popularity or prosperity. If we want to set our aim on success, lasting success, it might be wise to aim for experiencing the "true life" that is described here and in the letter to Timothy. What do you think that might be?

____

____

True life can be found by experiencing the power of the Holy Spirit unleashed in our work and relationships. Might these relationships be the purpose for our work since they are the one thing that last forever?

Our work creates the space for us to worship God, serve Him and others. The money we make allows us to build further relationships, creating more impact. The impact we have, our lasting success, is defined by how well we love others while we are here.

Group Discussion:
How might this view of success change the interactions you have on a daily basis with your co-workers, clients and leadership? What if you treated each interaction with this Kingdom perspective?

____

____

Relationships are all around you on a daily basis, opportunities to build into your eternal treasures. Set your aim on investing into them. It is how you can find purpose in your work and lasting success. As we continue on our journey, we will be diving into Kingdom relationships and how to further unleash God's power in them.

Challenge for the week:
Spend some quiet time with God reflecting on your view of relationships. How would you treat others differently if you knew you were building eternal friendships? Who is someone you can invest in over the next 6 months?

Prayer Requests:

Memory Verse

Here's the lesson: Use your worldly resources to benefit others and make friends. Then, when your possessions are gone, they will welcome you to an eternal home.

Luke 16:9

Unleashed
Section 2
Building Kingdom Relationships in Your Work

KINGDOM RELATIONSHIPS

SESSION 1

KINGDOM VIEW

Opening Discussion:

During the first section of *Releasing Power and Purpose in Your Work*, we talked about Simon Peter and his fishing excursion. In the story Peter experienced incredible success in his work, catching fish, but at the end of the story, it wasn't catching fish that Jesus called Peter to continue doing.

> *Then Jesus said to Simon, "Don't be afraid; from now on you will fish for people." So they pulled their boats up on shore, left everything and followed him.*
>
> Luke 5:10-11

Jesus shares that in following Him, Peter will be fishing for people. Each of us are called to do the same. Long after the work we contribute is gone, the love we showed through our relationships will remain. It is the one legacy we have to leave and the one thing that goes with us when we leave. Relationships built on God's love are the way we join in bringing God's Kingdom to Earth. That is why we are calling them Kingdom relationships. They are for here and now, and also for eternity.

Even if we understand the eternal impact our interactions with people at work can have, we often don't take the time to really foster them. Why do you think that is?

____

____

What is one of your most memorable relationships you have experienced over the course of your career? Why was it so impactful?

____

____

Relationships are hard work and how someone else responds to us or treats us is completely out of our control. For this reason, we cannot look to our own ability as our source for building Kingdom relationships. We need to unleash the power of the Holy Spirit to help us love in all circumstances. It is only through God's power, we can offer love to all those we encounter in our day.

> *Dear friends, let us love one another, for love comes from God. Everyone who loves has been born of God and knows God. Whoever does not love*

does not know God, because God is love. This is how God showed his love among us: He sent his one and only Son into the world that we might live through him. This is love: not that we loved God, but that he loved us and sent his Son as an atoning sacrifice for our sins. Dear friends, since God so loved us, we also ought to love one another. No one has ever seen God; but if we love one another, God lives in us and his love is made complete in us.

1 John 4:7-12

God loves us so we ought to love one another. There is a natural flow of love coming from God into each of us and then back to God and out to others. Sounds perfect. While God's love to me IS perfect, my love to others is far from that. Unfortunately the breakdown occurs when we try and love from our own ability. We all fall short and hurt others or they hurt us.

Group Discussion:
What would it look like for us to express the same love we receive from God? What holds you back from letting His love flow freely through you?

____

____

The filter or lens in which we view others is created by experiences we have had personally or witnessed through others. This creates a world view which can impact our ability to let God's love flow through us. Today we want to look at some of these world views and how we might shift them to a Kingdom perspective. Once we eliminate some of the filters, we can be open to releasing the power of the Holy Spirit in our relationships.

NOT AT WORK **World view:** Work is just my job. I do it because I have to in order to support myself and, or my family. Relationships are not part of the equation, and they get in the way of getting the job done.

Kingdom view: Relationships are one of the main purposes of my work. They are the one thing that lasts forever. Every interaction has the ability to transform a life.

FEAR

World view: If I open my heart and love and care about a co-worker, I will be setting myself up to be hurt. I am afraid to be so vulnerable. What if they use it against me?

Kingdom view: *"When I am afraid, I will trust in you."* Psalm 56:3
When we trust that God will protect us, we can give love freely without fear.

SCARCITY

World view: Work already takes up so much of my energy. Relationships can be very draining. I won't have enough for my friends and family.

Kingdom view: There is an endless supply when we look to God as our source to fill us. *"The grace of our Lord was poured out on me abundantly, along with the faith and love that are in Christ Jesus."* 1 Timothy 1:14

JEALOUSY

World view: Their life is so perfect. They are the favorite one who can do no wrong. They don't need me.

Kingdom view: You have no idea what they are really going through. Some of the most put together people are the loneliest.

WORTHY

World view: My position isn't high enough to be in relationship with them. Or they are not good enough to be in relationship with me because they have not achieved what I have.

Kingdom view: You are both made in the image of God, so you are both worthy because of Him.

RECIPROCAL

World view: If they are nice to me, then I will be nice to them.

Kingdom view: *"We love because he first loved us."* 1 John 4:19. Because God loved us first, we are able to love others.

Group Discussion:
What world view do you need to change in order to let God's love flow freely in and through your life?

____

____

If we unleash the power of the Holy Spirit into our relationships, our perspective will shift to the Kingdom view, and we will find ourselves seeing others as God does. Then from this new perspective, His love will flow freely into our hearts then overflow out to others. Unleashing the Holy Spirit in our lives is how we fulfil Jesus' command to love one another as He loved us.

Challenge for the week:
Spend some time this week reflecting on when you hold back showing love and compassion for those around you. Ask yourself why you are choosing to withhold God's love. What would the Kingdom view be in the situation and how might the Holy Spirit help you respond with God's love?

Prayer Requests:

KINGDOM RELATIONSHIPS

SESSION 2

ROMANS 12

Opening Discussion:
Last session we talked about how unleashing the power of the Holy Spirit in our relationships can help us shift our viewpoint to the Kingdom view and experience loving our co-workers the way Jesus intended. The love of God will flow freely into our hearts and out of our hearts to others. Kingdom relationships are built on this love.

How do you feel about releasing God's love into your work relationships? How do we do it? What would be the advantage of doing so?

____

____

Paul gives us some great ideas for actions we can take to build Kingdom relationships. As we read the following scripture, underline some of his instructions.

> *Love must be sincere. Hate what is evil; cling to what is good. Be devoted to one another in love. Honor one another above yourselves. Never be lacking in zeal, but keep your spiritual fervor, serving the Lord. Be joyful in hope, patient in affliction, faithful in prayer. Share with the Lord's people who are in need. Practice hospitality.*
>
> *Bless those who persecute you; bless and do not curse. Rejoice with those who rejoice; mourn with those who mourn. Live in harmony with one another. Do not be proud, but be willing to associate with people of low position. Do not be conceited.*
>
> *Do not repay anyone evil for evil. Be careful to do what is right in the eyes of everyone. If it is possible, as far as it depends on you, live at peace with everyone.*
>
> Romans 12:9-18

Group Discussion:
Reviewing what you underlined, how have you successfully enacted any of these in your workplace? Is there any area in particular that you struggle putting into practice?

____

____

Jesus experienced everything we will in our relationships, the good, the bad and the downright hateful. Not only did He show us how to handle each situation, He also gave us His power to do the same. However, unleashing it, that is still our choice. Paul provides instructions for us based on how Jesus lived. Over our next seven sessions, we are going to unpack Romans 12 and learn how putting it into practice can help us unleash the power of Kingdom relationships in our work.

Foundation of Trust: Lasting relationships must begin with a foundation of trust, which is gained through our actions over time. When we are authentic, vulnerable and consistent with how we treat others around us, we will earn their trust.

Authenticity—*Love must be sincere.* Vulnerability— *Do not be proud.* Consistency—*Never be lacking in zeal, but keep your spiritual fervor.*

Discover how each interaction you face during your day is an opportunity to demonstrate your love for others and earn their trust.

Value the Team: Paul says, *"Be devoted to one another in love."* How well do you love your team and each member of it? Do you find yourself including only certain team members in decisions? Discover the benefits of valuing the contributions of each team member and how together we can accomplish more than we can individually.

Managing Conflict: Paul says, *"Live in harmony with one another. If it is possible, as far as it depends on you, live at peace with everyone."* It's inevitable when we are on a team and working alongside others, we will encounter conflict. How can we view conflict as a healthy part of our relationships? Could God allow conflict in your relationships for a bigger purpose? Discover what it means to be a peacemaker instead of a peacekeeper when conflict arises.

Handling Rejection: Paul says, *"Bless those who persecute you; bless and do not curse. Do not repay anyone evil for evil."* We can try our best to love others and care for them, but sometimes, things don't work out. Jesus experienced a great deal of rejection as He offered the Kingdom to everyone who would listen. How well do you handle rejection or criticism? What happens when you are passed over for a promotion? Discover how to handle rejection with a Kingdom perspective and release any negative emotion that you might hold from past hurts.

Honor: Paul says, *"Honor one another above yourselves."* In relationships, we certainly don't always get our way. There are times when we need to step back and put our co-workers interest above our own. Are you able to remove your emotion from the situation and look at it from a different lens? Discover how to look at others the way God sees them and speak words of love and kindness.

Empathize: Paul says, *"Rejoice with those who rejoice; mourn with those who mourn."* When we empathize, we must remove ourselves from the center of our thinking. When someone else succeeds, are you envious or do you celebrate? What about when they fail? Do you point out their faults or feel the pain with them? Relationships that last mean we are there, walking beside each other no matter what. We pause and offer our presence right where they are without solving.

Sharing: Paul says, *"Share with the Lord's people who are in need. Practice hospitality."* Your journey in learning to build Kingdom relationships is not meant for you alone. It should be shared with others. Who is in need of your help? How can you build into someone that shows them how much God cares for them? You always have something you can offer no matter what position you hold.

Group Discussion:
Is there any particular topic that stirs emotion in you for any reason? Which one and why?

____

____

Your work, it is important, but the relationships you build, the people you meet along the way, that is what really matters. Relationships are hard work, take a lot of time and sometimes feel like they offer nothing in return. Don't forget, you aren't doing this on your own, you have the power of the Holy Spirit in you. When you unleash It into your relationships, there will be lasting impact. You never know, the two minute interaction you have with someone later today might change their life forever. With Jesus, people were changed by just touching the hem of his garment. Who will be changed by your interactions?

Challenge for the week:
Spend some quiet time with God reflecting on your relationships at work. How important are they to you today? How might God be asking you to consider going deeper into your relationships and unleashing His love to those around you?

Prayer Requests:

KINGDOM RELATIONSHIPS

SESSION 3

FOUNDATION OF TRUST

Opening Discussion:
Romans 12 emphasizes the importance of relationship. Kingdom relationships are built on a foundation of trust.

What is the importance of trust in the workplace? Does it exist in your current culture?

____

____

Describe some of the characteristics of people whom you trust. What makes them trustworthy?

____

____

How do you feel when you have to trust an unreliable person to help you with something? What makes them untrustworthy?

____

____

> *Putting confidence in an unreliable person is like chewing with a toothache or walking on a broken foot.*
>
> Proverbs 25:19

We certainly don't want to put our trust in an unreliable person, and hopefully, we are not the unreliable one. Successful teams are built on relationships, and strong relationships have a foundation of trust. Understanding how we can contribute to building trust is important to unleashing Kingdom relationships in our workplace.

In Brené Brown's book *Dare to Lead*, she illustrates trust using marbles in a jar. She says, "We trust the people who have earned marbles over time in our life. Whenever someone supports you, or is kind to you, or sticks up for you, or honors what you share with them as private, you put marbles in the jar...Those are the folks you trust with information that's important to you."

Every interaction we have throughout our day is an opportunity to contribute marbles into someone's jar. One marble at a time, we can build our foundation of trust. How do we contribute marbles? Recall from Paul's letter to the Romans, "Love must be sincere." Sincerity and trust go hand in hand. We can demonstrate this in our relationships through our authenticity, vulnerability and consistency over time.

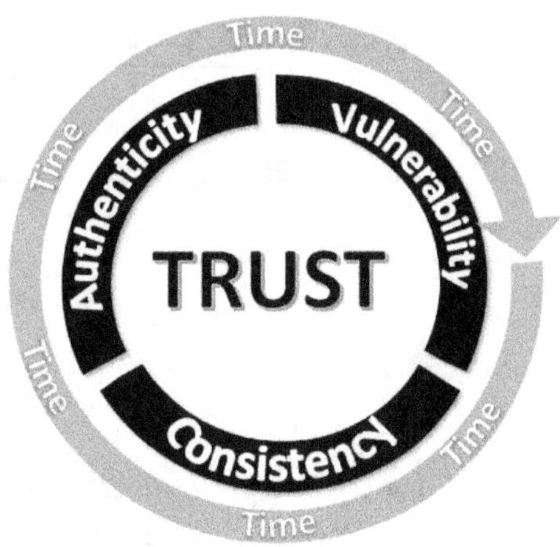

◊   Authenticity: Honest, transparent and genuine; ability to be yourself
◊   Vulnerability: Share weaknesses, fears and mistakes
◊   Consistency: Treat everyone equally, keep commitments and follow through

AUTHENTICITY

Author Brené Brown says, "Authenticity is the daily practice of letting go of who we think we're supposed to be and embracing who we are."

Who or what defines who you think you are supposed to be?

____

____

What if we allowed our Creator to define who we are? How would that impact our relationships? Here are a few things He says about who you are:

For you created my inmost being; you knit me together in my mother's womb. I praise you because I am fearfully and wonderfully made; your works are wonderful, I know that full well.

Psalm 139:13-14

For we are God's masterpiece. He has created us anew in Christ Jesus, so we can do the good things he planned for us long ago.

Ephesians 2:10

How would believing these truths help you be your authentic self? What impact would that have on your relationships?

____

____

VULNERABILITY

Vulnerability is often a scary concept for us. We spend a lot of time building the walls up around us so no one will think we are weak or know we are afraid.

How comfortable are you with being vulnerable at work? Why? Why is vulnerability even necessary with people at work?

____

____

And so it was with me, brothers and sisters. When I came to you, I did not come with eloquence or human wisdom as I proclaimed to you the testimony about God. For I resolved to know nothing while I was with you except Jesus Christ and him crucified. I came to you in weakness with great fear and trembling. My message and my preaching were not with wise and persuasive words, but with a demonstration of the Spirit's power, so that your faith might not rest on human wisdom, but on God's power.

1 Corinthians 2:1-5

How does Paul's vulnerability help build a foundation of trust?

____

____

CONSISTENCY

Trust is not built on a single event. When our behavior or reaction is consistent from day to day, it makes us more reliable and builds trust.

Jesus provides a great example of this for us to model:

> *Jesus Christ is the same yesterday and today and forever.*
>
> Hebrews 13:8

How consistent are your words and actions? Do you follow through when you say you are going to do something?

____

____

How does consistency help build our foundation of trust in relationships?

____

____

Challenge for the week:
If we are going to unleash Kingdom relationships, we might want to begin putting into practice the ways we can build trust with our work teams. Now is a good time to put it all together and commit to making changes moving forward.

One thing I will do differently to be more of my authentic self:

____

____

One thing I will do differently to be more vulnerable:

____

____

One way I will practice being more consistent:

____

____

Prayer Requests:

KINGDOM RELATIONSHIPS

SESSION 4

VALUE THE TEAM

Opening Discussion:
Much of our discussion up until this point has been about the one on one relationship dynamic in our workplace. This week, we will be looking at our relationships as it pertains to being a member of a team. This can often bring diversity of thought and personality, as well as skillset and ability.

Share with the group one of the best experiences you have had on a team. Describe some of the details including how many people were on it, what the function was and what made it so good.

____

____

Why are teams important? Why do you think most workplaces operate in teams?

____

____

In Romans 12, Paul tells us to *"be devoted to one another in love."* Are you devoted to your current work team? How about the individual members? Why or why not?

____

____

> *Two are better than one, because they have a good return for their labor:*
> *If either of them falls down, one can help the other up. But pity anyone*
> *who falls and has no one to help them up. Also, if two lie down together,*
> *they will keep warm. But how can one keep warm alone? Though one*
> *may be overpowered, two can defend themselves. A cord of three strands*
> *is not quickly broken.*
>
> Ecclesiastes 4:9-12

Group Discussion:
What can this scripture teach us about the value of a team?

____

____

Just as a body, though one, has many parts, but all its many parts form one body, so it is with Christ. For we were all baptized by one Spirit so as to form one body—whether Jews or Gentiles, slave or free—and we were all given the one Spirit to drink. Even so the body is not made up of one part but of many.

*Now if the foot should say, "Because I am not a hand, I do not belong to the body," it would not for that reason stop being part of the body. And if the ear should say, "Because I am not an eye, I do not belong to the body," it would not for that reason stop being part of the body. If the whole body were an eye, where would the sense of hearing be? If the whole body were an ear, where would the sense of smell be? **But in fact God has placed the parts in the body, every one of them, just as he wanted them to be.** If they were all one part, where would the body be? As it is, there are many parts, but one body.*

*The eye cannot say to the hand, "I don't need you!" And the head cannot say to the feet, "I don't need you!" On the contrary, those parts of the body that seem to be weaker are indispensable, and the parts that we think are less honorable we treat with special honor. And the parts that are unpresentable are treated with special modesty, while our presentable parts need no special treatment. **But God has put the body together,** giving greater honor to the parts that lacked it, so that **there should be no division in the body, but that its parts should have equal concern for each other.** If one part suffers, every part suffers with it; if one part is honored, every part rejoices with it.*

1 Corinthians 12:12-26

Group Discussion:
What can this scripture teach us about the value of a team?

____

____

The body operates interdependently. Each part relies on the others to function as it should so they work perfectly together. Do your teams operate the same way? Do you work independently or interdependently? What is an example of each one?

____

____

Our scripture says *"God has put the body together,"* and that He "placed them just as He wanted them to be." Have you ever considered that God has put each individual on your team for a purpose? Strong, weak, emotional, tough, analytical, risk taker, all of them, exactly where He wanted them to be, working with you. How would this Kingdom viewpoint change how you valued each member of the team?

____

____

"My prayer is not for them alone. I pray also for those who will believe in me through their message, that all of them may be one, Father, just as you are in me and I am in you. May they also be in us so that the world may believe that you have sent me. I have given them the glory that you gave me, that they may be one as we are one— I in them and you in me— so that they may be brought to complete unity. Then the world will know that you sent me and have loved them even as you have loved me. "

John 17:20-23

Group Discussion:
Jesus is praying not only for our unity with Him and The Father, but also with each other here on earth. Unity of the body is not only meant for church, but also in our work. How can you help bring this unity to the teams you affect?

____

____

Challenge for the week:
Think about the members of your team. How are you valuing each member for the unique contribution they bring? Consider sharing positive feedback for each member this week as a way to build Kingdom relationships with them.

Prayer Requests:

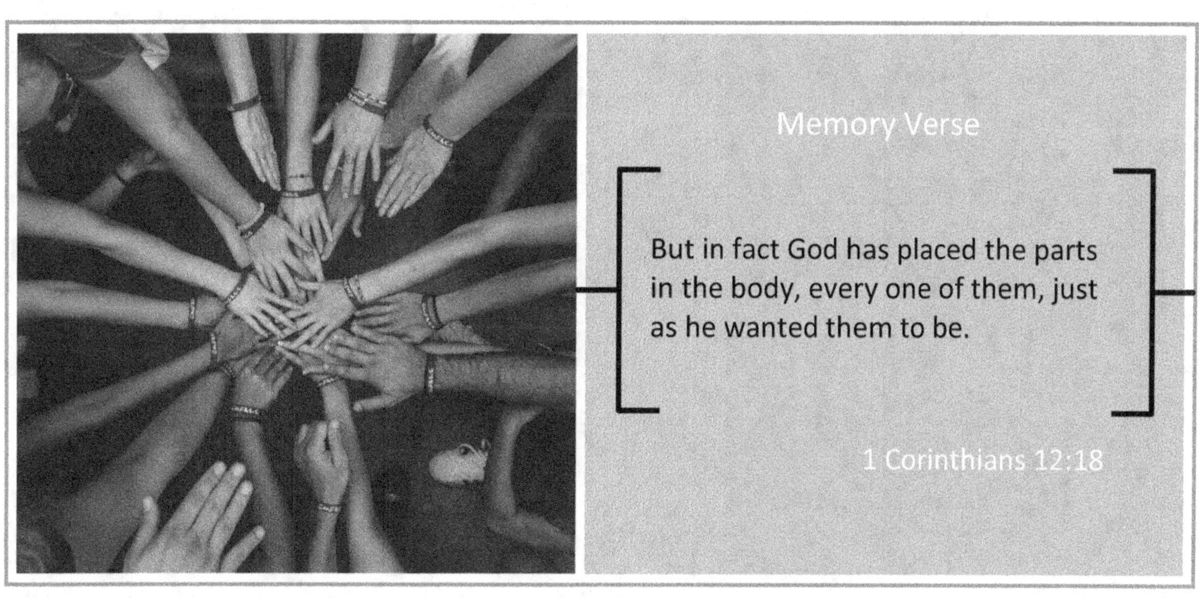

Memory Verse

But in fact God has placed the parts in the body, every one of them, just as he wanted them to be.

1 Corinthians 12:18

KINGDOM RELATIONSHIPS

SESSION 5

MANAGING CONFLICT

Opening Discussion:
Last session we discussed how unleashing the power of the Holy Spirit into our relationships at work helps us value each member of our team and work together as one. Working with others, interacting with people who have different personalities or those who think differently or act differently than we do is often the hardest thing we do at work. We each have our own story which creates a filter from which we perceive the moments of our life. In this session, we will be looking at the dynamics of these relationships and the conflict that sometimes occurs as a result. We will also seek to understand how conflict can be healthy and why we should embrace it.

How do you feel about facing conflict? Do you typically avoid it, manage it or create it? Give an example of how you have handled a recent conflict at work.

____

____

When we hear the word "conflict," we tend to focus on the single definition of the word – "fight, battle, war" as defined in the *Merriam-Webster Dictionary.* However, conflict can be a very good thing and is even necessary for us to achieve our full potential.

Let's review the conflict continuum below and discuss how becoming a peacemaker might help us build Kingdom relationships in our work.

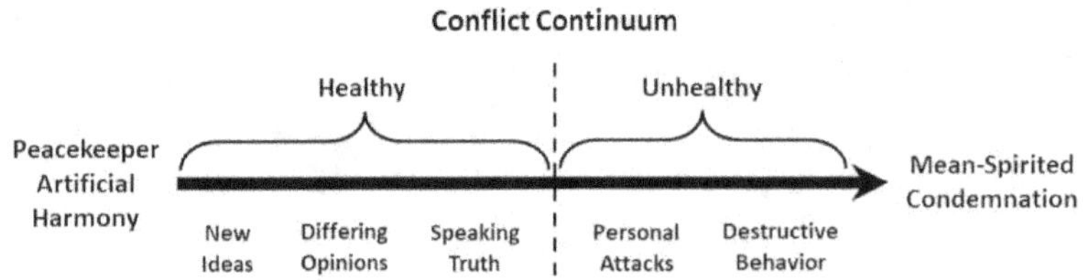

On the far left is the Peacekeeper. They promote artificial harmony. They are the conflict avoiders and will pretend like everything is fine no matter how dysfunctional the team is becoming.

Group Discussion:
Why might being a peacekeeper be more harmful than good?

____

____

The various types of conflict on our continuum span from healthy to unhealthy and even destructive behavior. Starting with healthy conflict, valuing new ideas and differing opinions brings about the best solutions to the team. When we are not open to these, we miss the unique contribution each member brings to the team.

Speaking truth is next and there is a very fine line between this and personal attacks. When we speak truth, it should be from a place of love and through a trusting relationship. Unhealthy conflict occurs when personal attacks and destructive behavior takes place. Unleashing the power of the Holy Spirit into these situations can help bring about a positive outcome in the midst of pain.

Jesus said:

> *Blessed are the peacemakers, for they will be called Children of God.*
> Mathew 5:9

Peacemakers exist all along our conflict continuum. They help bring out the new ideas and differing opinions from team members. They know how to speak truth and can bring healing when unhealthy conflict occurs.

What is the difference between a peacekeeper and a peacemaker?

____

____

Ken Sande, author of *The Peacemaker—A Biblical Guide to Resolving Personal Conflict*, says "Peacemakers are people who breathe grace. They draw continually on the goodness and power of Jesus Christ, and then they bring His love, mercy, forgiveness, strength, and wisdom to the conflicts of daily life."

Ken's description of a peacemaker sounds a lot like how we have described unleashing the power of the Holy Spirit into our relationships. There is action in being a peacemaker. That action might be building others up who are experiencing conflict, initiating restoration in relationships or speaking truth to a brother or sister.

Peacemakers build others up:
God calls us to use conflict as an opportunity to build others up in their time of need.

*So then we pursue the things which make for peace and the **building up** of one another.*

Romans 14:19 NASB

*Let no corrupting talk come out of your mouths, but only such as is good for **building up**, as fits the occasion, that it may give grace to those who hear.*

Ephesians 4:29 ESV

The peacemaker is found in each of these scriptures building others up. They bring the grace and peace of Jesus Christ into all situations.

How have you used conflict as an opportunity to build someone up?

____

____

Peacemakers initiate restoration:
In Romans 12 Paul reminds us, *"Live in harmony with one another. If it is possible, as far as it depends on you, live at peace with everyone."* Make every effort to live at peace means sometimes we have to GO and restore broken relationships, whether it is our fault or not.

*If your brother sins against you, **go** and tell him his fault, between you and him alone.*

Matthew 18:15 ESV

*So if you are offering your gift at the altar, and there remember that your brother has something against you, leave your gift there before the altar and **go**. First be reconciled to your brother, and then come and offer your gift.*

Matthew 5:23-24 ESV

How have you offered forgiveness to someone in your work? What did you do to restore the relationship?

____

____

Peacemakers speak truth:
Fear of conflict can keep us from speaking truth to our team and co-workers. Paul tells us speaking truth helps your team grow.

> *Rather, speaking the truth in love, we are to grow up in every way into him who is the head, into Christ, from whom the whole body, joined and held together by every joint with which it is equipped, when each part is working properly, makes the body grow so that it builds itself up in love.*
> Ephesians 4:15-16 ESV

How have you experienced conflict making your team stronger and closer in relationship?

____

____

Challenge for the week:
Spend time talking with God how you can be a better peacemaker. Where in your work is a peacemaker needed? What does it look like?

Practice building others up and bringing the grace of Jesus into conflict this week.

Prayer Requests:

KINGDOM RELATIONSHIPS

SESSION 6

HANDLING REJECTION

Opening Discussion:
While Kingdom relationships last forever, here on earth, most of our relationships have a life-cycle. When they end abruptly or outside of our control, it can feel like rejection. When we are passed over for a promotion or left out of an important discussion, it can feel like rejection.

Share a time when you faced rejection in your work. What happened and how did you respond to it? Do you tend to fight back or flee when you feel rejected?

____

____

What does it look like to unleash the power of the Holy Spirit to help us handle the rejection we face? In Romans 12 Paul says, *"Bless those who persecute you; bless and do not curse. Do not repay anyone evil for evil."*

Our tendency might be to reject those who reject us. Left to our own abilities, that is sometimes the easiest response. It might also be to seek revenge, speak poorly of the person, or harbor bitterness and anger towards them. When Jesus was facing people in towns that did not want anything to do with him, He would just walk away.

> *They got up, drove him out of the town, and took him to the brow of the hill on which the town was built, in order to throw him off the cliff.* ***But he walked right through the crowd and went on his way.***
>
> Luke 4:29-30

Group Discussion:
What would it look like to have the power to be unaffected by rejection? Why do you think Jesus could walk right through? What keeps us from being able to move through these situations the way He did?

____

____

Jesus knew who He was and what His purpose was on earth. He had the confidence to walk right through situations like this unaffected. If that seems impossible for you, let's look at a story of Jesus sending out the seventy-two with instructions on how to handle rejection:

"When you enter a house, first say, 'Peace to this house.' If someone who promotes peace is there, your peace will rest on them; if not, it will return to you.

Stay there, eating and drinking whatever they give you, for the worker deserves his wages. Do not move around from house to house.

"When you enter a town and are welcomed, eat what is offered to you. Heal the sick who are there and tell them, 'The kingdom of God has come near to you.' But when you enter a town and are not welcomed, go into its streets and say, 'Even the dust of your town we wipe from our feet as a warning to you. Yet be sure of this: The kingdom of God has come near.'

Whoever listens to you listens to me; whoever rejects you rejects me; but whoever rejects me rejects him who sent me."

Luke 10:5-11, 16

Group Discussion:
Why did Jesus instruct them to even wipe the dust from their feet as they walked away? How can we do the same when we are faced with rejection in the workplace?

____

____

In the scripture, Jesus tells them to stay in the house that welcomes them, where their needs are being met, and not to move around from house to house. What might this mean for us today as it relates to our jobs?

____

____

Have you ever feared being rejected by your leadership at work? If so, how does this fear affect your work and health? How about confidence level? What if we worked with the attitude that as long as we are welcome, we will do our job to the best of our ability and then when it is time to move on, we will pick up our stuff and go?

____

____

When Jesus came into this world, even some of His closest followers rejected Him when He did not meet their expectations or when they feared for their own lives.

Even when betrayed by one of His own disciples, He didn't lose sight of the plan for His life. If Jesus is not rejected and crucified, the Kingdom does not come, and we are not restored to our right relationship with God.

> *And he said, "The Son of Man must suffer many things and be rejected by the elders, the chief priests and the teachers of the law, and he must be killed and on the third day be raised to life."*
>
> Luke 9:22

Looking at rejection from a Kingdom perspective means we put aside our hurt feelings and seek to understand God's plan and purpose in the midst of it. The world would tell us the rejection happened to you. God says it happened for you. Often times the new opportunity is better than what we imagined.

> *As the heavens are higher than the earth, so are my ways higher than your ways and my thoughts than your thoughts.*
>
> Isaiah 55:9

When is a time you felt rejected and later realized it was for the best and part of God's plan? Share your experience with your group.

____

____

Challenge for the week:
Reflect on a time when you felt rejected and God showed you a different path. Recount the fruit you experienced on that path. Take some time to sit and soak in thankfulness for the fruit and for the experience as a whole.

Consider any other rejection you might have not understood, and ask Him to show you His perspective and what you can learn from it.

Prayer Requests:

Memory Verse

As the heavens are higher than the earth, so are my ways higher than your ways and my thoughts than your thoughts.

Isaiah 55:9

KINGDOM RELATIONSHIPS

SESSION 7

HONORING OTHERS

Opening Discussion:
What does the word honor mean? We don't hear it used much in today's society outside of some wedding vows and something we should take time to do for various civil servants. Honor is defined by someone's importance or value, based upon virtue, excellence or character. Something that is set apart and treated with respect. Do you see honor in your workplace? What does honoring others look like?

In Romans 12:10, Paul instructs, *"Honor one another above yourselves."* Various interpretations are more emphatic about how we are to honor others:

> *In matters of worldly honor, yield to one another.—WNT*
> *Show eagerness in honoring one another.—NET*
> *Take delight in honoring each other.—NLT*
> *Outdo one another in showing honor.—ESV*

What comes to mind as you hear these scriptures? Do you believe you honor others well? What are some ways you can honor others in your workplace?

____

____

What are some things that prevent honor from being the default in how we interact with others?

____

____

Our own personal workload and stress can keep us focused internally and squeeze our time and energy for honoring others. However, sometimes co-workers or management can be mean-spirited, disrespectful or even condescending to us or others.

Why would it be even more important to treat them with honor? Is it possible? How?

____

____

In Matthew 19:26 Jesus told us "nothing is impossible with God." When we unleash the Holy Spirit in moments when words of anger and judgment are far easier and probably feel good to say, we will experience some of the most fruitful moments of our lives. Repeatedly the Bible describes the value of our words.

> *A gentle answer turns away wrath, but a harsh word stirs up anger.*
>
> Proverbs 15:1

> *Kind words are like honey-- sweet to the soul and healthy for the body.*
>
> Proverbs 16:24

Group Discussion:
Speaking with kindness is something we are raised to know. We've probably all heard, "If you don't have anything nice to say, don't say anything at all." What if we become counter culture and instead of unleashing words of anger or remaining silent, we ask the Holy Spirit to use us to speak kindness and gentleness? Can you think of an instance where this might have made a positive difference in a work situation?

____

____

As he wrote to the Romans, Paul must have felt honoring others was very important. He nestled it between two vital instructions: devotedly loving one another and serving the Lord. Why is the order of his instructions important? Could Paul have been saying that we must be devoted to genuinely loving others so any words we speak or action we take to honor another person is out of the overflow of love and not an empty action? Therefore, these actions are how we can serve the Lord.

> *If I could speak all the languages of earth and of angels, but didn't love others, I would only be a noisy gong or a clanging cymbal.*
>
> 1 Corinthians 13:1

> *But love your enemies, do good to them, and lend to them without expecting to get anything back. Then your reward will be great, and you will be children of the Most High, because he is kind to the ungrateful and wicked.*
>
> Luke 6:35

Group Activity:
Why is God kind to the ungrateful and wicked? Is it possible for us to do the same? How can we genuinely love that co-worker who stabbed us in the back or the boss who belittled us in front of our peers?

Let's pause for a moment and do a visualization exercise. Close your eyes. Imagine the person as a child, 3 or 4 years old, expanding in new experiences daily and discovering the world. The experiences of life haven't marred them in any way. They are full of potential and hope. Can you love that child, that child who is the seed of God's dream, created in His image? Somewhere along the way things happened that formed the person you know. Life's ups and downs can refine us or become events that define us.

What would happen if you spoke words or did the things you felt the Holy Spirit guiding you to say or do out of an overflow of love for this child?

____

____

The Bible mentions honor in many places. It tells us honor our parents, our bodies and that all of creation honors Jesus. These types of examples might be easier to put into action. Paul's letter to the Romans expands this to others, not just our parents, self and Jesus. Peter makes a similar statement:

> *Honor **all** people, love the brotherhood, fear God, honor the king.*
>
> 1 Peter 2:17

Group Discussion:
Peter said ALL people should be honored, not just kings, but all mankind. WHY? Why is this concept of honoring others from God to parents to kings to every person so important?

____

____

Imagine a home, a workplace, a community where everyone knew they were made in the image of God. Where everyone acted as though they were image bearers. Where everyone loved and treated others in a way that honored the image of God within them. Can you imagine such a place? We, as believers, not only are image bearers, but we are also a temple of His dwelling. We carry God IN us. What if we are in the position we are in to bring God into that space? What if we are being asked to unleash the Holy Spirit not just into a specific space, but around specific people? What if treating others with honor, out of the over flow of God's love within us, is the key that helps open them up to considering that they are a child of the Most High God and made in His image as well? Thus, creating a place for the Holy Spirit to begin working on their heart and mind to discover their true identity.

Challenge for the week:
Take some time to think about those you honor and those you don't. Spend time visualizing the child they once were and ways you can begin to honor them. Visualize asking the Holy Spirit to help you in those tough moments. Tell the Holy Spirit that you want to unleash Its power through you to others, ask for help in knowing HOW. Ask for ears that can hear the instruction clearly so you can honor others out of the love that God pours into you.

Prayer Requests:

KINGDOM RELATIONSHIPS

SESSION 8

EMPATHIZE

Opening Discussion:

Last session we talked about honoring others above ourselves. Another way we can do this is to place ourselves alongside someone else and feel what they are feeling in their circumstances. Paul says in Romans 12:15, *"Rejoice with those who rejoice; mourn with those who mourn."*

How well do you empathize with people in your workplace? What is an example of a time when you found yourself celebrating someone's success or sharing their heartbreak because of a failure?

____

____

Why is it important to empathize with others? What are some of the benefits you have experienced?

____

____

Clearly, our Heavenly Father saw empathy as important because He sent His Son into the world to become flesh and walk among us, to feel and experience life exactly the way we do. He didn't have to come. He could have saved us without doing this. Why do you think He chose to experience our humanity with us?

____

____

> *For we do not have a high priest who is unable to empathize with our weaknesses, but we have one who has been tempted in every way, just as we are—yet he did not sin.*
>
> Hebrews 4:15

Jesus teaches us how to empathize with others by showing us through His own example. Therefore when we see others in need, we should in turn walk alongside them. Remember how we discussed God's love flowing through us and into others? Our ability to comfort others in their time of need follows this same flow:

Praise be to the God and Father of our Lord Jesus Christ, the Father of compassion and the God of all comfort, who comforts us in all our troubles, so that we can comfort those in any trouble with the comfort we ourselves receive from God.

2 Corinthians 1:3-4

The experiences you have in life are not only shaping you, they also allow you to relate to others and help them in their time of need.

Group Discussion:
When have you experienced comfort from God? How has it allowed you to empathize with someone else in their time of suffering?

____

____

Our ability to empathize, or understand the feelings of another, is possible even when we haven't experienced the exact same situation. One way to do this is to imagine yourself in place of the other person. How are they feeling? Can you relate to the emotion they are feeling in the moment? While the situation might look differently, the emotion is probably something you have felt before. In this moment of empathy, God connects one heart to another and there is a bonding that takes place. This is how Kingdom relationships are created. It can happen without words or trying to fix the situation. Just an understanding, almost as if you are sharing one mind and one body. Isn't this how it should be if we are all members of one body through Christ?

If one member suffers, all suffer together; if one member is honored, all rejoice together.

1 Corinthians 12:26

Sometimes it is easier to comfort someone when they are struggling or have experienced failure than to rejoice or celebrate someone else's success. Why do you think we might struggle with this, especially at work?

____

____

There are certainly times when rejoicing comes easy. Our friend at work gets a big promotion, our team reaches our goal or someone we mentored experiences success. In the Gospel of Luke, Jesus says *"if we love those who love us, what credit is it to us?"* In the same way, if we rejoice only with those who rejoice with us or are part of our team, what good is that? It certainly wouldn't require us to unleash any power outside of our own ability to do so.

David understands how hard it can be to rejoice when others are successful and shows us to seek God's help:

> *Fill my heart with joy when **their** grain and new wine abound.*
>
> Psalm 4:7

Rejoice with those who rejoice, even when it is someone who is unkind, hard to love or difficult to be around. Proverbs warns us,

> *Don't rejoice when your enemies fall; don't be happy when they stumble,*
> *or the Lord will see and disapprove.*
>
> Proverbs 24:17-18a NLT

Group Discussion:
How could empathy help us with those in our lives who are more difficult? What would need to take place for us to be able to relate to how they are feeling in the moment and share their joy or pain?

____

____

Challenge for the week:
Make space in your day to notice what is going on around you. Who doesn't seem like themselves this week? Perhaps it's someone in your staff meeting, in the kitchen or walking past you in the hallway. What might they be going through that isn't being shared? Allow the Holy Spirit to connect your heart to theirs and get a sense for the emotion they are feeling. Make time to pull them aside and ask how they are doing. Then listen. Ask the Holy Spirit to guide you in the moment.

Prayer Requests:

Memory Verse

If one member suffers, all suffer together; if one member is honored, all rejoice together.

1 Corinthians 12:26

KINGDOM RELATIONSHIPS

SESSION 9

SHARING

Opening Discussion:

Throughout our time together we have been unpacking Romans 12 and how it can help us build Kingdom relationships. Much of our discussion has been around some tough topics like conflict, rejection and putting others above ourselves. We pour into others to build trust, mend relationships and show their value as a child of God. So much giving of ourselves to build into others. This relationship business is hard work. So why do we do it? Do we exist to only serve the needs of others? What's in it for us?

Have you ever felt exhausted from relationships and wondered if they were really worth all the effort? Why do we continue to pursue them?

———————————————————————————————————————

———————————————————————————————————————

Our last instruction from Paul in regard to relationships is about sharing. He says, *"Share with the Lord's people who are in need. Practice hospitality."*

Who is in need? What should we be sharing with them? **Everyone** is in need, and we **all** have something to share. What is it?

———————————————————————————————————————

We can share our money, food, clothing, talents and those are all very good things, but what people really need is YOU. We need each other. We need to be in relationship and community. That's why we work so hard to build and maintain relationships. Our Father and Jesus want the same relationship with them and with each other.

> *"As the Father has loved me, so have I loved you. Now remain in my love. If you keep my commands, you will remain in my love, just as I have kept my Father's commands and remain in his love. I have told you this so that my joy may be in you and that your **joy may be complete**. My command is this: **Love each other as I have loved you**. Greater love has no one than this: to lay down one's life for one's friends. You are my friends if you do what I command. I no longer call you servants, because a servant does not know his master's business. Instead, **I have called you friends**, for everything that I learned from my Father I have made known to you. "*

> John 15:9-15

Group Discussion:
Are your co-workers servants or friends? What is an example of each?

____

____

Jesus calls us friends and challenges us to be in relationship with others. Today we are going to look at some of the reasons why we would want to build into relationships and how they might benefit us. After all, "The LORD God said, 'It is not good for the man to be alone. I will make a helper suitable for him.'" - Genesis 2:18

BRINGS JOY

Jesus says in John 15 that our joy is made complete through loving relationships with Him and each other.

John reiterates Jesus' words:

> *We proclaim to you what we have seen and heard, so that you also may have fellowship with us. And our fellowship is with the Father and with his Son, Jesus Christ. We write this **to make our joy complete**.*
>
> 1 John 1:3-4

Reflection: Think about a relationship you have that brings you joy. Sit in that feeling for a moment.

LIGHTENS YOUR LOAD

Trying to face life's challenges alone can be very heavy and lead to stress and anxiety.

> *Carry each other's burdens, and in this way you will fulfill the law of Christ.*
>
> Galatians 6:2

Reflection: Remember a time when someone helped you. Capture how that felt and hold onto that for a moment.

IMPROVES DECISIONS

Bringing plans to a group of trusted friends helps us find the best solutions.

Plans fail for lack of counsel, but with many advisers they succeed.

Proverbs 15:22

Reflection: Remember a time when someone helped you make a decision. How would things be different if they hadn't been there?

REFINEMENT

A smaller subset of friends who know us better can help mold and shape us.

As iron sharpens iron, so one person sharpens another.

Proverbs 27:17

Reflection: Think about a friend who challenged you to improve in an area of your life. How have they had a positive impact on you?

BRINGS ENCOURAGMENT

It's easy to give up when difficulties come. Relationships provide strength and encouragement when we need it most.

And let us consider how we may spur one another on toward love and good deeds, not giving up meeting together, as some are in the habit of doing, but encouraging one another—and all the more as you see the Day approaching.

Hebrews 10:24-25

Reflection: Remember a time when a friend came along side you at a difficult time and provided the encouragement you needed to keep going. How did it feel to be cared for in this way?

Group Discussion:
Thinking back through your reflection, what stood out to you about the benefit of relationships and sharing your life with others?

____

____

Each of these benefits are part of developing Kingdom relationships and forever friends. Cherish the moments you have with co-workers, clients and leaders because they are momentary interactions that have eternal impact.

Challenge for the week:
Review your notes from this week's study. Who is someone who has had an impact on your life? If possible, make time to reach out to them this week and share how they have made a difference.

Prayer Requests:

Unleashed

Section 3
God's Plan for the Good Life

THE GOOD LIFE

SESSION 1

INTRODUCTION

Opening Discussion:
How would you describe the *good life*?

____

____

> *I remain confident of this: I will see the goodness of the LORD in the land of the living.*
>
> Psalm 27:13

Did you know you had the ability to see the fullness of God here on earth? How many times have you prayed the Our Father and spoken the words, *"Your kingdom come, your will be done, on earth as it is in heaven."*? This is how Jesus taught us to pray. What do those words mean?

Seeing the Kingdom come here to your daily life is possible and that is the good life. Unfortunately, we don't experience this on a daily basis because we have things that are blocking our view. Walls we have built up over time restrain and constrain the Holy Spirit from flowing freely which places limits on the ability we have to fully experience the good life God has planned for us.

We think of walls as protection. Walls are safe because they keep a threat out, the bigger the better! However, from the inside, it can be a fortress that keeps people in, limits movement or even imprisons. Individually, we put up walls to protect us from pain, but that wall is then a prison of sorts for the Holy Spirit that lives inside of us.

Group Discussion:
What are some things that constrain the Holy Spirit from flowing freely? Can you identify any wall you might have up and why it is there?

____

____

Jesus came and showed us how to live freely without walls. He showed us what it looks like for the Kingdom to come to earth. He knew we would need a Helper to give us strength to let down our walls and experience the goodness of the Lord in our lives.

Nevertheless, I tell you the truth: it is to your advantage that I go away,
for if I do not go away, the Helper will not come to you. But if go, I will
send him to you.

John 16:7

Throughout our time together, we are going to focus on some of the walls or constraints we have put on the power to live like Jesus taught us. We hope to uncover what holds us back from experiencing the fullness of the Spirit in our lives, the good life God planned for us. Before we look at the individual constraints, we should consider the key to the main gate which holds the Holy Spirit captive. What do you think it would be? What would help you overcome fear, doubt, uncertainty and hardship?

Trusting God. Do you fully trust God? Do you trust He is good? He is faithful? He is unchangeable? He has good plans for you? He wants what is best for your future?

"For I know the plans I have for you," declares the Lord, "plans to
prosper you and not to harm you, plans to give you hope and a future."

Jeremiah 29:11

God is Love, He is Faithful, He is Unchangeable, He is Constant and His mercies are new every morning. Therefore, God is worthy of our trust. Our lack of trust in God is the root of all the constraints that keep us from unleashing the Holy Spirit fully in our lives and living the good life He dreamed for us.

Why is trusting God often so hard to do?

____

____

When we trust God, and unleash His Spirit to move freely in and through our lives, constraints are released into the fruits of the Spirit. We have this hope because faithfulness, the unchangeable nature of God, is part of His trustworthiness.

But the Holy Spirit produces this kind of fruit in our lives: love, joy, peace,
patience, kindness, goodness, faithfulness, gentleness, and self-control.
There is no law against these things!

Galatians 5:22-23

Group Discussion:
Which fruit of the Spirit do you find difficult to maintain consistently in your life?

____

____

Challenge for the week:
Spend time thanking Jesus for sending the Holy Spirit. Talk to Him about all the reasons why it's so hard for you to trust. Before the Holy Spirit was sent, in Luke 17, the apostles/disciples asked for more faith. We, too, can ask to be filled with faith. This comes to us through the Holy Spirit. Ask Jesus to show you how you constrain the Holy Spirit in your life. Ask God's Holy Spirit to come and fill you anew, and to give you the faith you need to trust God so that you are able to unleash the fruits of His character in your life.

Prayer Requests:

THE GOOD LIFE

SESSION 2

RELEASE PLANS

Opening Discussion:
How many times have you spent hours planning something only to have it not come to pass or be completely ruined by some unforeseen factor? How does that disappointment feel? Why? This session we will be discussing the constraint of focusing on our own plans, and how trusting in God's plans releases patience.

When we have a plan in mind, what grows in our hearts is an expectation. Think of "the plan" as the outcome and logistics to accomplish it and "the expectations" as a combination of the motivation and emotions you have invested into it. Whether or not we plan out of something we hear from God to do or simply something we have desired in our heart to do, when it does not come to fruition as we had planned or hoped, we are disappointed and even hurt. Ultimately these disappointments affect our trust in God.

Take a few moments to share with the group a time when you have felt disappointment when things didn't turn out as you had planned. Do you see any connection to this event and your trust in God? If so, how?

____

____

> *Many are the plans in a person's heart, but it is the LORD's purpose that prevails.*
>
> Proverbs 19:21

> *There is a way that seems right to a man, but its end is the way of death.*
>
> Proverbs 16:25

Group Discussion:
What's the difference between our plans and the Lord's purpose?

____

____

Have you ever prayed about a situation and asked God what to do, and when you heard an answer, you took it and ran with it? Does this always work out? How can a way that seems right end up falling apart? Why do you think that happens?

____

____

What if the reason that the plan fails even if we heard them from God is because we didn't wait for the "HOW" and "WHEN"? God has a strategy and purpose for all things. Strategies only *begin* with "what." For them to be successful, there has to be timed steps to the process. *"We can make our plans, but the LORD determines our steps."* —Proverbs 16:9

> *I will instruct you and teach you in the way you should go; I will counsel you with my loving eye on you.*
>
> Psalm 32:8

> *The LORD will guide you **continually**, giving you water when you are dry and restoring your strength. You will be like a well-watered garden, like an ever-flowing spring.*
>
> Isaiah 55:11

God, our loving creator, doesn't just want to tell us what to do and have us run off and do it. He wants to walk it out with us. He desires to be a part of it with you instructing, teaching, guiding and counselling you along the way, keeping His loving eye upon you!

Group Discussion:
What are some of the benefits of walking out the plan with God?

____

____

What is the main constraint that keeps us from taking advantage of these benefits? Here is a clue: Have you ever been on a road trip and heard the words, "are we there yet?" Patience, or lack of it, has probably sent us down many wrong paths.

How can trusting God to give us patience to wait on His timing instead of making it happen on our own? Can you think of a time when God's timing has proven to be different from what you expected?

____

____

> *Trust in the Lord with all your heart, and do not lean on your own understanding. In all your ways acknowledge him, and he will make straight your paths.*
>
> Proverbs 3:5-6

The shortest distance between two points is a straight line. The shortest distance between God giving us the plan and it happening can also be a straight line when we walk the path with Him. Otherwise, we begin meandering back and forth wondering which way to go and questioning if we even heard from God in the first place. Trust God and His timing. He has a better view:

> *For my thoughts are not your thoughts, neither are your ways my ways, declares the Lord. For as the heavens are higher than the earth, so are my ways higher than your ways and my thoughts than your thoughts. "For as the rain and the snow come down from heaven and do not return there but water the earth, making it bring forth and sprout, giving seed to the sower and bread to the eater, so shall my word be that goes out from my mouth; it shall not return to me empty, but it shall accomplish that which I purpose, and shall succeed in the thing for which I sent it.*
>
> Isaiah 55:8-11

When the Lord brings the full plan, His plan, we can have confidence that as we follow His instructions, walk through it with Him, it will be better than we could have ever planned on our own. There is no need to strive to get it done. No pressure to meet a deadline. We gain patience in our trusting Him in His plan, so much so that time is no longer a factor.

It's like going on a hiking adventure with your best friend and an experienced guide. You can enjoy the journey. There is no need to worry about the plans for which path you will take or how long it will take to get there. Arriving at the final destination might be the goal, but enjoying the time together on the journey is part of the purpose for the trip. Removing the expectations and pressure of getting to the goal will allow you to experience the good life God has planned for you.

Group Discussion:
Do you believe looking at your plans in this way will bring patience? What is one insight you have taken away from today's discussion or scriptures?

____

____

Challenge for the week:
Make a list of some of the plans you believe God has for you or ones that are desired in your heart. Spend time asking God "when" and "how" each one is planned to come to fruition.

What is His timing? What are the next steps you can take together?

Prayer Requests:

THE GOOD LIFE

SESSION 3

RELEASE CONTROL

Opening Discussion:
We have been talking about letting down our walls so that we can unleash the Holy Spirit into our work and relationships. Today, let's focus in on the "leash" part of "unleashing." When do we use a leash and how might that relate to these constraints we have been discussing?

The single greatest purpose of a leash is to restrain an animal or control it. When we say something is on a "tight leash," we are keeping it even closer, more tightly held. Our desire for controlling situations, people or our own future, can put a significant constraint on the power of the Holy Spirit working in our lives.

Take a minute and consider how you typically respond in the following situations. Place a "X" on the scale for when you generally are the one in control or if others are:

Situation	Self———---Others
Project needs completed at work, who volunteers to lead?	
Meeting is getting off track, who reigns it in?	
Something goes wrong, who fixes it?	
Do you ask others to help or do most tasks yourself?	

How controlling are you? There are some situations where it is easier to let go and other times when we hold on much more tightly. What is something you are trying to maintain control over in your work? Why do you feel the need to control or own it?

____

____

Attempting to be in constant control of our lives is not only exhausting, it is a major source of stress and anxiety. Why do you think stress is an outcome of control?

____

____

How does trusting in the Lord help us overcome our stress and anxiety?

____

____

Control is a restraint that says, "God, I've got this." This wall not only keeps the Holy Spirit from being unleashed in your work, it also prevents relationships from forming. Control ultimately comes down to who you trust: self over other and self over God.

When we release our control to God, we are putting our trust in Him and believe He will help us because He cares for us.

> *Cast all your anxiety on him because he cares for you.*
>
> 1 Peter 5:7

> *Give your burdens to the Lord, and he will take care of you.*
>
> Psalm 55:22

Group Discussion:
What would it look like to release control to God? Is that even possible?

____

____

What fruit of the Spirit do you receive when you release control of your anxiety and worry?

____

____

When chaos is happening around us, we have a tendency to try to grasp onto the control of more things, only increasing our realization of how little we are actually controlling. When we let go in these moments and hand it over to God, we experience the fruit of **peace**, even in the midst of uncertainty. Removing the wall of control unleashes the Holy Spirit into our hearts and minds to silence the chatter.

> *Do not be anxious about anything, but in every situation, by prayer and petition, with thanksgiving, present your requests to God. And the **peace** of God, which transcends all understanding, will guard your hearts and your minds in Christ Jesus.*
>
> Philippians 4:6-7

Group Discussion:
"By prayer and petition, with thanksgiving"...what does this look like in our lives? How have you experienced the fruit of peace when you have made known your requests to God?

____

____

Group Exercise:
What would it look like to live our lives in a complete trust of God to be in control, without worry and stress? How would we feel?

Take a moment and close your eyes. Think about the situation that came to mind earlier today when we asked where you were trying to maintain control or something that feels out of control. Take three deep breaths in and release each one slowly.

Prayer: Invite the Holy Spirit to come and join you in the stillness. Have a conversation with Him about what's on your heart.

Petition: Make your request known to God about how you would like Him to help in the situation.

Thanksgiving: Praise Him for what He has already done and what He will do through it.

Take one more deep breath and release with an "amen."

How do you feel?

____

____

When we trust God and hand every situation over to Him, we will live a life of peace. This is the good life God has planned for you.

> "But blessed is the one **who trusts in the LORD**, whose confidence is **in Him**. They will be like a tree planted by the water that sends out its roots by the stream. It does not fear when heat comes; its leaves are always green. It has no worries in a year of drought and never fails to bear fruit."
> Jeremiah 17:7-8

No matter what comes your way, you will be like a tree, standing firm and deeply rooted, no worries, bearing the fruit of peace.

Challenge for the week:
Releasing control to someone involves a great deal of trust. It is easier to trust someone when you know them well, and they know you. Throughout the Bible names were used to show a person's function. There are many beautiful names of God that describe the detailed ways in which He reveals Himself to us, so we can put our trust in Him.

> And those who **know your name** put their **trust in you**, for you, O Lord,
> have not forsaken those who seek you.
>
> Psalm 9:10

Turn to pages 136-137 to find a list of 'Names for God'. Take a few moments and circle two or three that resonate strongly within you.

Meditate on how knowing God in a more personal way helps you release control and trust in His plans which ultimately brings you peace.

Be prepared to share one name you chose and why.

Prayer Requests:

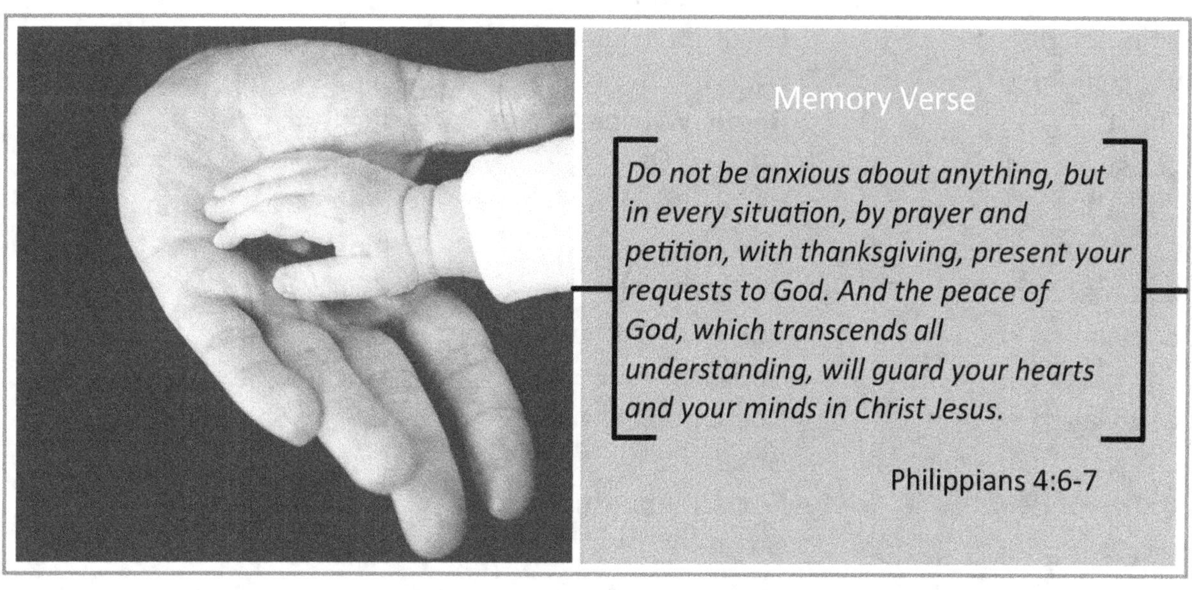

Names for God

Abba	Defender	Great High Priest
Advocate	Deliverer	Great Shepherd
Almighty	Desired of all Nations	Guide
All in All	Door	Head of the Body
Alpha	Dwelling Place	Head of the Church
Amen	Elect One	Heir of All Things
Ancient of Days	Emmanuel	Hiding Place
Anointed One	End	Highest
Architect	Eternal God	High Priest
Author of Eternal Salvation	Eternal Life	High Priest Forever
Author of our Faith	Eternal Spirit	Holy Ghost
Author of Peace	Everlasting Father	Holy One
Avenger	Everlasting God	Holy Spirit
Banner	Excellent	Hope
Beginning	Faithful & True	Horn of Salvation
Blessed & Holy Ruler	Faithful Witness	Husband
Branch	Father	I AM
Bread of Life	Father of Lights	Immanuel
Breath of Life	Firstborn	Intercessor
Bridegroom	First Fruits	Jealous
Bright Morning Star	Fortress	Jehovah
Carpenter	Foundation	Jesus
Chief Shepherd	Fountain of Living Waters	Jesus Christ our Lord
Chosen one	Friend	Judge
Christ	Gentle Whisper	Just one
Christ of God	Gift of God	Keeper
Christ the Lord	Glory of the Lord	King
Comforter	God	King Eternal
Commander	God Almighty	King of Glory
Consuming Fire	God of the Whole Earth	King of Jews
Cornerstone	God Over All	King if Kings
Counselor	God who Sees Me	King of Saints
Creator	Goodness	Lamb of God
Crown of Beauty	Good Shepherd	Last Adam
Dayspring	Governor	Lawgiver

Names for God

Leader
Life
Life Giver
Light of the world
Like an Eagle
Lily of the Valleys
Lion of the Tribe of Judah
Living God
Living Stone
Living Water
Lord
Lord God Almighty
Lord God of Hosts
Lord Jesus Christ
Lord of All
Lord of Glory
Lord of Harvest
Lord of Lords
Lord our Righteousness
Love
Lovingkindness
Maker
Majesty on High
Man of Sorrows
Master
Mediator
Merciful God
Messenger of the Covenant
Messiah
Mighty God
Mighty One
Most Upright
Nazarene
Offspring of David
Omega

Omnipotent
Omnipresent
Omniscient
One
Only Begotten Son
Our Passover Lamb
Our Peace
Physician
Portion
Potter
Prince of Life
Prince of Peace
Prophet
Prophet of the Highest
Protector
Provider
Purifier
Quickening Spirit
Rabbi (teacher)
Radiance of God's Glory
Redeemer
Refiner's Fire
Refuge
Restorer
Resurrection
Rewarder
Righteous one
Rock
Root of David
Rose of Sharon
Ruler of God's Creation
Ruler Over Kings of Earth
Ruler Over Israel
Safety
Savior

Scepter
Seed
Servant
Shade
Shelter
Shepherd of our Souls
Shield
Shiloh
Song
Source
Sovereign
Spirit
Spirit of Adoption
Spirit of God
Spirit of Truth
Star out of Jacob
Strength
Stone
Stone of Israel
Stronghold
Strong Tower
Teacher
Temple
The One
True Light
True Witness
Truth
Vine
Wall of Fire
Way
Wisdom of God
Witness
Wonderful
Word
Yahweh

THE GOOD LIFE

SESSION 4

RELEASE FEAR

Opening Discussion:
Our challenge last week was to spend some time thinking about the names of God and getting to know Him better so we can release control and unleash peace in our lives. What was one of the names of God that you circled and why?

____

____

Perhaps one of the reasons we struggle with control is based on an underlying fear that we won't have enough. We don't trust God will supply our needs, so we try to do it on our own. The Lord spoke to Jeremiah and said:

> *"My people have committed two sins:*
> *They have forsaken me, the spring of living water,*
> *and have dug their own cisterns, broken cisterns that cannot hold water."*
>
> Jeremiah 2:13

While today we might not fear running out of water, there are plenty of areas where we fear scarcity, so we take matters into our own hands. If we believe God is who He says He is, we can trust that He will provide for us.

Where do you fear not having enough? How are you dealing with the fear?

____

____

Taking control of the situation ourselves might help us reduce the fear associated with it. However this is often temporary, or as we talked last session, can create a lot of stress and anxiety. Trusting God is really the only way to receive peace. How do we eliminate the fears around areas of our life that are completely out of our control? How do you overcome fears related to illness, loss of job or even death?

Did you ever wake up in the middle of the night as a child and feel afraid? What did you do to eliminate the fear?

____

____

One of the immediate things a child in fear desires is the closeness of a parent. Just as a parent reassures a child there is nothing to fear, God does the same for us:

*"Be strong and courageous. Do not be afraid or terrified because of them, for the Lord your God goes with you; **he will never leave you** nor forsake you."*

Deuteronomy 31:6

Just like a parent to a child, God says, "do not be afraid, I am here and will never leave you." He is ALWAYS with us. How? Through the Holy Spirit. If we release our fear to God and trust that He is with us, we can receive His love.

God's love has been poured out into our hearts through the Holy Spirit, who has been given to us.

Romans 5:5b

The Spirit you received does not make you slaves, so that you live in fear again; rather, the Spirit you received brought about your adoption to sonship. And by him we cry, "Abba, Father." The Spirit himself testifies with our spirit that we are God's children.

Romans 8:15-16

Group Discussion:
How have you known God as Father in your life? How has this helped you in times of fear? If you have not experienced God as Father, why do you think that is?

____

____

"God's love has been poured out into our hearts through the Holy Spirit." This love, if we are able to receive it, casts out fear and allows us to experience the good life God has planned for us.

There is no fear in love, but perfect love casts out fear. For fear has to do with punishment, and whoever fears has not been perfected in love.

1 John 4:18

How does love eliminate fear? How would trusting God produce the spiritual fruit of love?

____

____

[35]Who shall separate us from the love of Christ? Shall trouble or hardship or persecution or famine or nakedness or danger or sword? [36]As it is written:

"For your sake we face death all day long;
we are considered as sheep to be slaughtered."

*[37]No, in all these things we are more than conquerors **through him who loved us.** [38]For I am convinced that neither death nor life, neither angels nor demons, neither the present nor the future, nor any powers, [39]neither height nor depth, nor anything else in all creation, will be able to separate us from the love of God that is in Christ Jesus our Lord.*

Romans 8:35-39

In the beginning of this scripture, Paul talks about some of the fears the people of this time experienced: trouble, hardship, persecution, famine, nakedness, danger or sword. Let's replace this list with some of the fears you are allowing to occupy space in your life right now. What is on your list?

____

____

Which of these fears shall separate you from the love of God? None of these things. Read the second part of the scripture again. Nothing can separate us from God's love except our own walls we put up inside our heart. Releasing this wall, unleashes the possibility for us to fully experience God's love poured into our hearts. You are a dearly loved child of God. Receive it.

Challenge for the week:
Pray and reflect on the following:

Make a list of fears that you have in regard to your answer in the final question of our discussion. Meditate on God's love and Romans 8:37-39. Ask God to help you replace these fears with His love poured into your heart.

Prayer Requests:

Memory Verse

God's love has been poured out into our hearts through the Holy Spirit, who has been given to us.

Romans 5:5b

THE GOOD LIFE

SESSION 5

RELEASE DOUBT

Opening Discussion:
Last session we talked about releasing fear and receiving the fruit of God's love through the Holy Spirit. We find this referenced again in a verse from Paul to Timothy:

> *For God did not give us a Spirit of fear but of power and love and self-control.*
>
> 2 Timothy 1:7 NET

We see love and self-control as two of the gifts of the spirit found in Galatians 5:22-23. One we talked about last session and the other we will be looking at next session. But what about "power"? Which fruit of the spirit might that bring and why?

> *But the Holy Spirit produces this kind of fruit in our lives: love, joy, peace, patience, kindness, goodness, faithfulness, gentleness, and self-control. There is no law against these things!*
>
> Galatians 5:22-23

____

____

Let's look at some scriptures where common people, like us, had the power to perform miracles, but doubt constrained their faith.

> *Immediately Jesus reached out his hand and caught him [Peter]. "You of little faith," he said, "why did you doubt?"*
>
> Matthew 14:31

> *Then Jesus told them, "I tell you the truth, if you have faith and don't doubt, you can do things like this and much more. You can even say to this mountain, 'May you be lifted up and thrown into the sea,' and it will happen."*
>
> Matthew 21:21

Group Discussion:
How has doubt put a constraint on the power of the Holy Spirit to be unleashed in your life?

____

____

Doubt can be overcome when we trust God and release our faith into the situation.

"Faithfulness," as it is referenced in Galatians 5, is not the same as God's character trait of faithfulness. The word used here is more readily defined as conviction of faith, assurance or belief in God. Faithfulness or our faith is a gift of the Holy Spirit. It is not by our own ability.

> *For it is by grace you have been saved, through faith—and this is not from yourselves, it is the gift of God.*
>
> Ephesians 2:8

How does Paul define "faith"?

> *Faith is the confidence that what we hope for will actually happen; it gives us assurance about things we cannot see.*
>
> Hebrews 11:1

Group Discussion:
Most of you probably have faith that God exists, but do you have faith that His plans for you are good? Do you have faith that what you hope for will actually happen? Why or why not?

____

____

Remember the plans we talked about in Session 2? Trusting God with them has a cascading affect on the other fruits as well. When we take control and make our own plans, we can experience fear of failure and can often begin to doubt ourselves and even our faith in God. Paul reminds us through faith we can have the confidence to hope for what God says will happen, will actually happen.

Let's consider the promises God has for us, and how they all come together to help us experience the good life with Him.

- ◊ He loves you. (Love)
- ◊ He goes before you in all you do. (Peace)
- ◊ There is hope in the days to come as you walk in them together. (Faithfulness & Patience)

First and foremost God loves you. He dreamt about you before you were even born. He created you and called you His child. There is no fear of what lies ahead for you because you are under His banner of love.

God also goes before you in all you do. There is no need to take control and map out the perfect plan for making your dream come to life. If He gave you the vision, He will make a way for it to happen. You can have peace in knowing that He is walking before you and showing you the way to go. He is the ultimate guide because He already knows where the pitfalls are on the journey and can help you navigate them. Every day of your life was recorded in His book. Every moment laid out before a single day passed. (Psalm 139:16)

He doesn't stop at just going before you. He wants to have a relationship with you, so He is also walking right beside you through it all. There is hope in the days to come because you are walking in them together. There is no reason to doubt or worry when things don't go exactly the way you thought they would. You can have faith that God has a reason and a purpose for every part of the journey, and the journey is actually part of the plan. It is meant to help you grow in relationship with your Father, gain patience in His perfect timing and prepare you for what's to come.

Group Discussion:
Share your thoughts on the freedom this would bring if we lived our lives in this way. Discuss the need for knowing the detailed plan, how it will work out and how long it will take.

____

____

Challenge for the week:
Reflect on the desires you have in your heart for plans in your life. Think about the difference between needing to know how and when they will happen vs. knowing God is with you on the journey. Adam and Eve ate from the tree of knowledge because they needed to know. God walking in the garden with them wasn't enough. They needed to see for themselves. How about you? Which is more important? Consider surrendering your plans to God and taking His hand to walk together. Feel the cool breeze in your face in the quiet of the day as you walk with Him. Talk with Him about what is on your mind. Seek Him, and His plans for your day. Rest in knowing it will be good.

Prayer Requests:

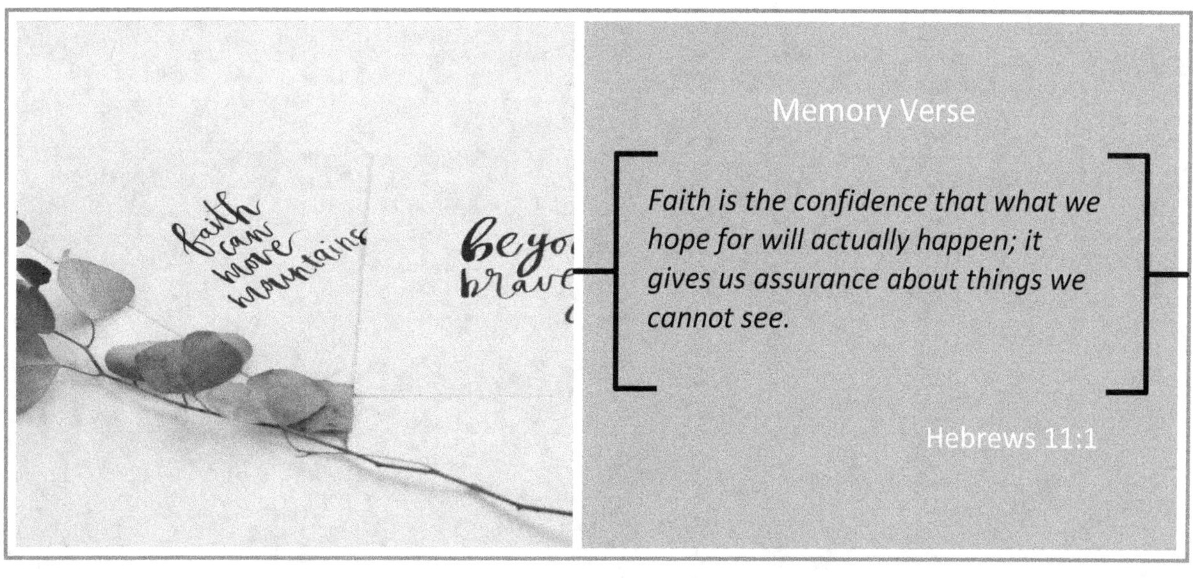
faith can move mountains
be yo
brave
Memory Verse
Faith is the confidence that what we hope for will actually happen; it gives us assurance about things we cannot see.
Hebrews 11:1

THE GOOD LIFE

SESSION 6

RELEASE BUSYNESS

Opening Discussion:
How often when you greet someone with, "How are you?" is the response, "busy"? And how often is the response, "exhausted!"? How can we possibly ALL be so busy? Has the pace of life encroached upon us while we weren't looking to keep us in state of constant doing? If we aren't physically doing something, our minds are racing with the list of what needs to be done, how and when we are going to do it and stressing about not having time to do it all. This busyness prevents us from seeing the goodness of the Lord in our lives and tends to leave us physically and mentally weary.

How busy are you on a daily basis? What does your schedule look like during the work day? How about the evening?

Bored out of your mind. 1   2   3   4   5   6   7   8   9   10   Can I be cloned?

Whether self-inflicted or not, in the midst of the countless responsibilities and obligations we have in order to serve others or support ourselves, how weary are you?

I could run a marathon. 1   2   3   4   5   6   7   8   9   10   Calgon take me away!

There is a story in the Bible about someone who was very busy, her name was Martha.

> *She had a sister named Mary, who also sat at the Lord's feet and was listening to what He said. But Martha was **distracted by her many tasks**, and she came up and asked, "Lord, don't You care that my sister has left me to serve alone? So tell her to give me a hand." The Lord answered her, "Martha, Martha, you are **worried and upset about many things**, but one thing is necessary. Mary has made the right choice, and it will not be taken away from her."*
>
> Luke 10:39-42 HCSB

Martha was very busy, not only with making dinner, but as Jesus pointed out, her mind was also busy worrying about her sister not contributing and more. Jesus said Mary made the right choice.

Group Discussion:
Do you feel like busyness is a choice? Why or why not?

____

____

How do we make the choice that Mary chose? Sitting at Jesus' feet and listening to what He says, learning what His voice sounds like. How do we tune out the expectations of the other voices?

Recall the verse we referenced last session about self-control.

> *For God did not give us a Spirit of fear but of power and love and self-control.*
>
> 2 Timothy 1:7 NET

Self-control is a fruit of the Spirit. It is what allows us to overcome our busyness and stand firm in our mind and actions, not to be pushed around by the expectations of the world around us.

Group Discussion:
What is the difference between "control" and "self-control"? How is one a constraint we have to release and the other one evidence of the Holy Spirit in our lives?

____

____

As we start to understand self-control as the power of the Holy Spirit inside us to help us make the right choice, we can release the self-inflicted busyness that comes from comparisons, distractions, or personal striving to make our plans happen the way we want in our timing. When we choose to wait on God's timing, we will find a renewed strength.

> *But they who **wait for the LORD** shall renew their strength; they shall mount up with wings like eagles; they shall run and not be weary; they shall walk and not faint.*
>
> Isaiah 40:31

Waiting for the Lord is key, and it takes a lot of self-control to wait. We discussed early on in our study how trusting God will bring us patience to let Him reveal *what* His plans are for us. The fruit of self-control will enable us to wait on *how* and *when* those plans are supposed to happen. It is hard to hold back when God has shown us the beauty of His plans. Remember He wants to go before us and walk beside us so running ahead of Him is not going to help us get there faster.

Group Discussion:
What does it look like to wait for the Lord's timing? How do we know when to move forward? How do we know which tasks are most important in our day?

____

____

Stopping and taking time to listen to God is the best way to understand what is important for us to do each day.

> *"Be still, and know that I am God. I will be exalted among the nations, I will be exalted in the earth!"*
>
> Psalm 46:10

When we are busy doing instead of being still, we are in essence exalting ourselves instead of allowing God to be exalted for what He is doing in our lives. Everything become urgent and we lose sight of what is most important.

What is your greatest constraint to making time with God? If you do have time with Him each day, how much of it is spent in stillness, listening? Why is this part as important, if not more essential, than reading our Bible and prayer?

____

____

Spending time with the Lord will renew us from our weariness, give us a new perspective and new motivation, bringing order to what *needs* to be done. Choosing to be still then asking the Holy Spirit for the self-control to stand fast in our choice and not be fickle is not just set aside for morning devotion. Practice this same self-control during a meeting or conflict. The stillness can be created in your mind throughout the day to hear God's voice. Listen for what He has to say, and trust that if something doesn't get done in the day that it wasn't supposed to happen, and it will be completed in His timing.

Challenge for the week:
This week, be diligent in making space in your schedule to be at Jesus' feet. Find a place to let go and be still. Each day, go apart from others where its quiet. Breathe. Connect with our Father, tell Him you want to learn to hear His voice. Tell Him you want to learn and know

that He is God, trustworthy to help you in the focus and pace your day. Ask Him to guide your schedule to focus on what and who is really important for that day and invite Him to walk through the day with you.

Prayer Requests:

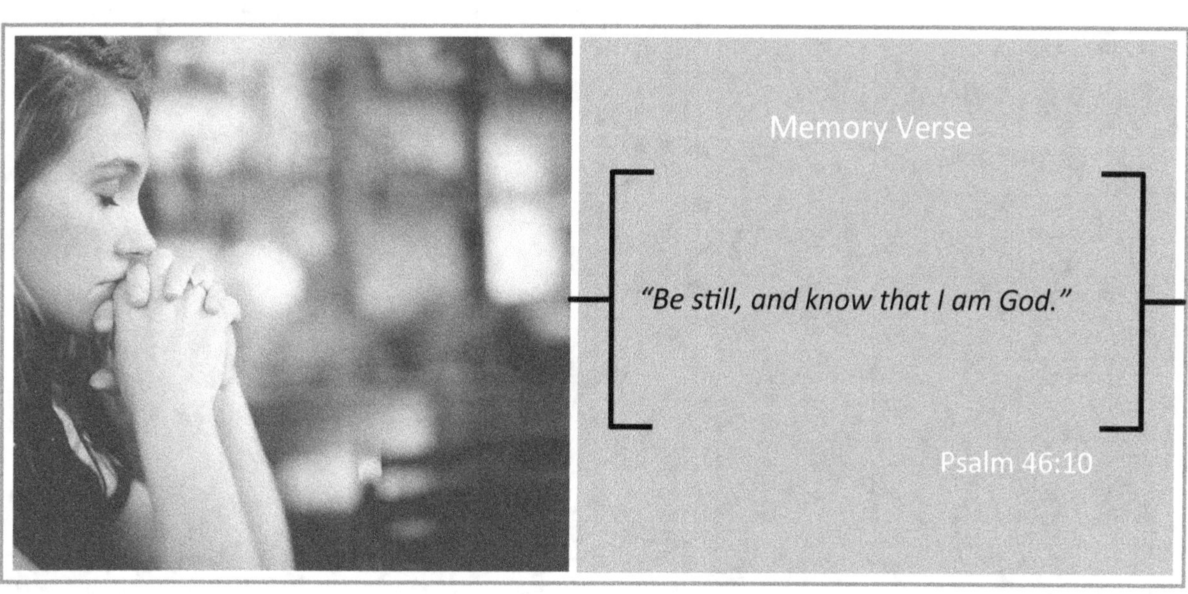

THE GOOD LIFE

SESSION 7

RELEASE DISCONTENTMENT

Opening Discussion:
Last session we discussed our busyness and how it hinders our ability to see the good life God has planned for us. One of the sources of our busyness is comparison and trying to keep up with others around us. We are bombarded in media with images of people having the newest car, clothing, house or gadget. We see people on vacation having fun on the beach or trekking through the mountains. We see people looking their best - beautiful makeup and perfectly fit. The expectation becomes that if we don't have what they have or look like them, then something is wrong with us.

We become discontent and begin to strive for something to satisfy our desires. What we compare ourselves to becomes a moving target that is unattainable because there is always the next shiny thing. Sometimes we achieve the goal only to realize we didn't even want it in the first place.

This constant striving has us in a state of stress, even if only in the back of our minds, where these comparisons and desires are a constant churn. When we get focused on them, they cause stress to our body, our mind and even our Spirit. They create discontentment in our lives.

Can you share areas in your life where you are experiencing discontentment? Are you able to identify why you are discontent?

____

____

Often times our desire to satisfy our discontentment causes us to become engrossed in striving for the next thing, and we lose sight of the goodness of God around us and constrain the Kingdom of God within us, which is the Holy Spirit. There is a war within our minds between the fulfillment of our want for worldly desires and our need for an intimate relationship with our Father. It is a battle for your heart and what fills it.

> *"Do not lay up for yourselves treasures on earth, where moth and rust destroy and where thieves break in and steal, but lay up for yourselves treasures in heaven, where neither moth nor rust destroys and where thieves do not break in and steal. For where your treasure is, there your heart will be also."*
>
> Matthew 6:19-21

Group Discussion:
What do you fill your heart with, what do you treasure? On what do you effortlessly spend your money and time? Is this a source of your discontentment?

____

____

When is what we have socially, mentally or physically ever good enough? How do we stop the noise around us from influencing us? Discontentment is a state of the heart. If we are discontented there is a conflict within us somewhere. How do we get to a place where we realize that we have all that we need? If we stop and think about it, we may find we have so much more of what we truly want as well.

Take a moment and think on the place(s) you thought about before that have you feeling discontent. Can you look at your life and see where you are striving for something that deep down isn't that important? Does something else you already have fill that desire? Are you actually thankful for what you do have, but just didn't realize it or forgot?

____

____

When we trust God to lead and direct us, He leads us to green pastures and quiet waters. Those waters are without pressure. Those green pastures are green with abundance and life.

> *The Lord is my shepherd, **I lack nothing**. He makes me lie down in green pastures, he leads me beside quiet waters, He refreshes my soul.*
>
> Psalm 23:1-3

This word "shepherd" means "to feed" and "tend to," but it is also translated as "companion" or "friend." When we allow God to be our companion in life, when we interact with Him as a friend, He will walk us into the plans He dreamed for us.

What God has for us is often different from what the influences around us lead us to believe we need. It isn't to say that He doesn't want us to have nice things or good titles at work or fun experiences, but what He has for us will last beyond a moment. God desires for you to lack nothing and experience the fullness of joy in this life, and it doesn't come with striving and pressure.

You make known to me the path of life; in your presence there is fullness
of joy; at your right hand are pleasures forevermore.

Psalm 16:11

Group Discussion:
What is joy? Do you remember the last time you were full of joy, not happiness, but real joy?
Share a time when you experienced it.

____

____

Here are a couple of instances from scripture where people experienced joy:

When they saw the star, they rejoiced with exceeding great joy.

Matthew 13:44

So they departed quickly from the tomb with fear and great joy, and ran
to tell his disciples.

Matthew 28:8

Both, interestingly, have to do with the life of Jesus. The star, a supernatural sign of the birth
of the Messiah, led them to the One who was to lead them out of bondage. This was a
spiritual event and something that was experienced within their spirits not just their flesh,
and joy was the result. The same is true for the mourning women when they had been told
that their beloved teacher and friend was not dead. Joy was the emotion that came when
there was life over death.

When we strive for the things of this world that will fade and essentially die along with us,
we are striving for death, and will live a life of discontentment. When we live life with God as
our shepherd and companion, we will find that we lack nothing and experience the fullness
of joy.

Group Discussion:
Can you imagine a joy-filled life? What does it look like?

____

____

Challenge for the week:
Make a list of the areas in which you are discontent, and the things you are striving to acquire or accomplish. Take each thing and ask God to take you to the quiet waters where the noise around you stops. Ask Him to show you what you already have that is truly what your heart desires. Ask what He has been trying to give you that you have not seen as desirable, but is indeed what will bear the fruit of joy in your life.

Prayer Requests:

163

THE GOOD LIFE

SESSION 8

RELEASE BLAME

Opening Discussion:

When we learn to trust God and let our walls down, the Holy Spirit can flow freely, and we start to experience fruits of love, joy, peace, patience and faithfulness. Life can feel pretty sweet. It can even start to begin to feel like we are invincible and nothing can trip us up. But we are still living in an imperfect world so something is guaranteed to go wrong, even when God is orchestrating the plans.

What is your immediate response when it does? Do you look for whose fault it is? Someone to blame? Do you ever blame Satan when things don't go the way you thought they should? Why do we look for someone or something to blame?

____

____

Let's look at the first recorded conversation of blame in our history. It goes all the way back to the beginning of humanity.

> *And he said, "Who told you that you were naked? Have you eaten from the tree that I commanded you not to eat from?"*
>
> *The man said, "The woman you put here with me—she gave me some fruit from the tree, and I ate it."*
>
> *Then the Lord God said to the woman, "What is this you have done?"*
> *The woman said, "The serpent deceived me, and I ate."*
>
> Genesis 3:11-13

Adam blamed Eve and Eve blamed Satan. Original sin released blame into existence, and we have been doing it ever since.

Today we are going to discuss how trusting God when things don't go as planned releases kindness and gentleness instead of blame and guilt. This lesson applies to how we treat ourselves as well as others.

> *For the entire law is fulfilled in keeping this one command: "**Love your neighbor as yourself**." If you bite and devour each other, watch out or you will be destroyed by each other.*
>
> Galatians 5:14-15

Paul is talking about loving each other instead of fighting and quarrelling. Blame works the same way and can not only destroy our relationships with others, but also how we treat ourselves. Since how we treat ourselves spills out to others, let's start our discussion with looking at how blame affects us individually.

Group Discussion:
What is the difference between taking ownership and blaming yourself? What does blame sound like in your head? How does it make you feel?

____

____

Is that what God would say about you? What do you think He would want us to say or do?

____

____

Our mistakes or times when we miss the mark do not define us. They are opportunities for us to learn and try again.

Have you ever felt the weightiness of sin in your life because you did something you felt was wrong? Did it feel like conviction or condemnation? Explain the difference.

____

____

If it resulted in blame, shame and prolonged guilt, then it was likely condemnation. When we release the power of the Holy Spirit, there should be no condemnation or blaming yourself:

> *Therefore, there is now **no condemnation** for those who are in Christ Jesus, because through Christ Jesus the law of the Spirit who gives life has set you free from the law of sin and death.*
>
> Romans 8:1-2

Because of the Holy Spirit living in us, we have no condemnation when we sin or miss the mark. Conviction, on the other hand, helps guide us back on the right path. We take ownership of what we did, return to God and keep walking. When we treat ourselves with the same kindness and gentleness that God gives us through His grace, we experience the good life He has planned for us.

> *Who will bring any charge against those whom God has chosen? **It is God who justifies.** Who then is the one who condemns? No one. Christ Jesus who died—more than that, who was raised to life—is at the right hand of God and is also interceding for us.*
>
> Romans 8:33-34

> *He has told you, O man, what is **good**; and what does the LORD require of you but to **do justice**, and to **love kindness**, and to **walk humbly with your God**?*
>
> Micah 6:8 ESV

We like blame because it justifies our feelings, but it is God who justifies, not us. We're told to do justice, which means we do what is right and leave judgment to God. Releasing blame removes the bitterness and anger that comes from injustice around us. Trusting God to be the ultimate judge allows us to choose forgiveness, kindness and gentleness. This is not by our power, but through the power of the Holy Spirt.

> *Let all bitterness and wrath and anger and clamor and slander be put away from you, along with all malice. **Be kind** to one another, **tenderhearted**, forgiving one another, as God in Christ forgave you.*
>
> Ephesians 4:31-32 ESV

Group Discussion:
How might viewing our shortcomings and those of others in this way help us replace blame with kindness and gentleness?

____

____

Challenge for the week:
Reflect on areas where you have had a tendency to place blame either on yourself or on others. Ask God to help you see it from His perspective. If there is something that needs corrected, ask the Holy Spirit to give you the strength and words to humbly return to the right path.

Prayer Requests:

Memory Verse

Let all bitterness and wrath and anger and clamor and slander be put away from you, along with all malice. Be kind to one another, tenderhearted, forgiving one another, as God in Christ forgave you.

Ephesians 4:31-32 ESV

THE GOOD LIFE

SESSION 9

THE GOOD LIFE

Opening Discussion:
Over this study we have identified some of the walls we have in our lives that are constraints for the Holy Spirit to release the fruits of the Spirit so we can experience the good life that God has planned for us. We have found through trusting Him and walking on the path with God, the goodness of the Lord is available to us here and now. Here is a reminder of where we started our discussion.

> *I remain confident of this: I will see the goodness of the LORD in the land of the living.*
>
> Psalm 27:13

Hopefully you have started to notice God walking with you, and your eyes have been opened to the goodness of the Lord around you. Does anyone have an example to share of how you have seen God differently as you have walked with Him?

____

____

Unleashing the Holy Spirit in our lives produces fruit. Which fruit of the spirit have you experienced through the time we have been studying Galatians 5?

> *But the Holy Spirit produces this kind of fruit in our lives: love, joy, peace, patience, kindness, goodness, faithfulness, gentleness, and self-control. There is no law against these things!*
>
> Galatians 5:22-23

____

____

Up until this point, we haven't discussed the last line of this scripture. This line represents the freedom we experience when we are walking in the fullness of the Spirit, no walls or constraints.

Do you believe this type of freedom is possible? What would it look like to live in a world where there were no laws needed?

____

____

Clearly, we haven't arrived at this place of freedom yet. We all struggle and fall short from time to time. That's ok. This life is a journey. It's God's plan for us to be transformed fully into His image, but it doesn't happen overnight.

> *And we all, with unveiled face, beholding the glory of the Lord, are being transformed into the same image from one degree of glory to another. For this comes from the Lord who is the Spirit.*
>
> 2 Corinthians 3:18

> *And he who searches hearts knows what is the mind of the Spirit, because the Spirit intercedes for the saints according to the will of God. And we know that for those who love God **all things** work together for **good**, for those who are called according to his purpose. For those whom he foreknew he also predestined to be conformed to the image of his Son.*
>
> Romans 8:27-29a

By letting our walls down, or removing our protective veil, we will be able to see how God is working all things together for good. All things we experience in this life are not good, but ALL THINGS work together for good. When we shift our perspective to looking at our life events through this lens, we will see how God is using our experiences to transform us into the image of Jesus. We will begin to understand that things are not happening to us, but for us. Everything happens for a reason, for God's will to be done here as in heaven.

Group Discussion:
Do you believe everything has a purpose? What about difficult life events? How have you experienced goodness when something bad happens to you or someone you love?

____

____

We notice from our first scripture that our transformation into the image of God happens one degree at a time. This is good news. God isn't asking for some radical change overnight. That means that He has no problem with how we are at the moment! He sees and knows the fullness of who we are becoming. All that matters is that we have turned to walk with Him. Each step is part of the overall plan and leads us closer to Him.

In addition, He is the one who does the work in us. We don't have to figure it out on our own! We simply need to be open to the Holy Spirit working in us.

*Being confident of this, that **he** who began a good work in you will carry it on to completion until the day of Christ Jesus.*

Philippians 1:6

You can be confident that God will never leave you along the journey. You will lack nothing. Put your trust in God and the plans HE has for you and experience the good life. The fruit of goodness represents living this good life, walking in the uprightness of heart and life.

Trust in the LORD and do good; dwell in the land and enjoy safe pasture.
Take delight in the LORD, and he will give you the desires of your heart.

Psalm 37:3-4

When we walk with God on this journey and do the good works He shows us along the way, we can experience the fullness of the Kingdom of God here on earth. Our heart begins to align with His heart, we delight in the loving relationship we have with Him, and we receive everything our heart desires.

Group Discussion:
Do you believe God's plan is to give you the desires of your heart? How could this be possible?

____

____

Challenge for the week:
Make a list of some of the ways you might be resisting the good life God has for you. What areas are you holding back from releasing to God? Take some time this week to pray and ask God to help you fully surrender and trust Him. Ask Him to align your heart to His and rest in knowing He is patient with you on the journey.

Prayer Requests:

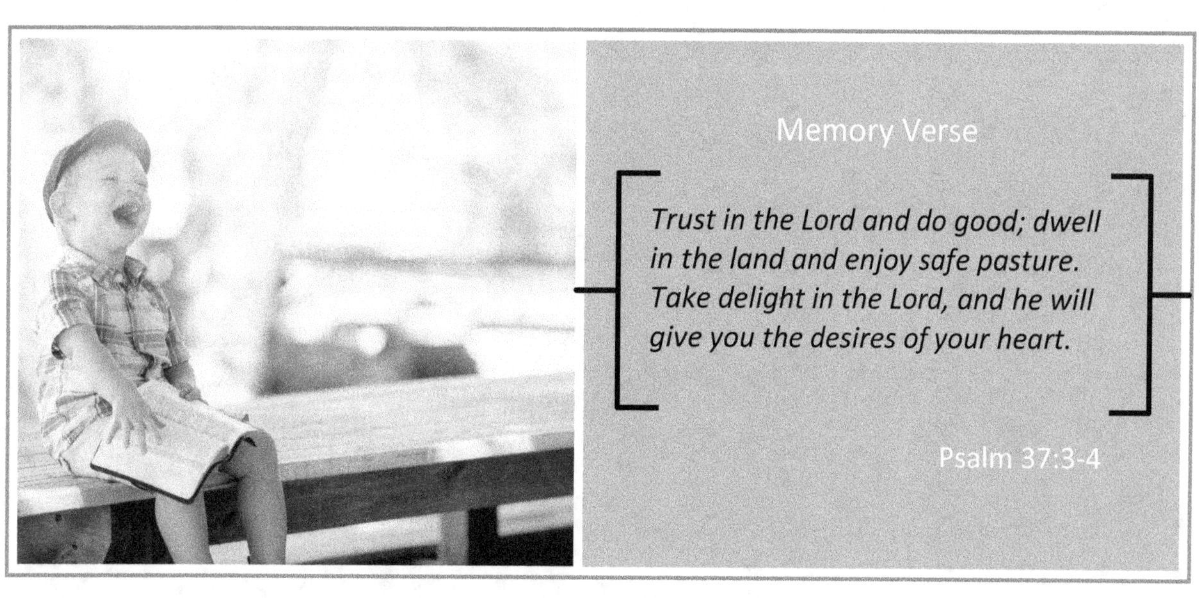

Memory Verse

Trust in the Lord and do good; dwell in the land and enjoy safe pasture. Take delight in the Lord, and he will give you the desires of your heart.

Psalm 37:3-4

THE GOOD LIFE

SESSION 10

NEXT STEPS

Opening Discussion:
Thinking back over our *Unleashed* journey, how have you experienced living a fully integrated life where the Holy Spirit flows freely whether you are at work, home or someplace else?

____

____

How has your perspective on the purpose for work and building kingdom relationships developed over our time together?

____

____

Now what? We hope that your newfound freedom and confidence from walking each day with God and trusting in His plan for you life will spark your interest in continued living with the Holy Spirit flowing freely in and through your life. We hope even more that you will help someone else with their journey. Help them find hope in the midst of believing work is supposed to be toil and just something we have to do while we are here. Help them experience the goodness of the Lord on earth as it is in heaven. Help them fully experience the gifts of the spirit and how to release them into their daily lives.

> *And do not forget to do good and to share with others, for with such sacrifices God is pleased.*
>
> Hebrews 13:16

Group Discussion:
Share an example of a time when you went through something and learned a lesson that you were later able to share with someone else who was going through a similar situation.

____

____

When you have the opportunity to do good, does it feel like a duty that you have to do or something you get to do? What is the difference? Give an example if you have one.

____

____

When we experience God's power and presence in our life, it is not intended solely for our own benefit. We find many examples in scripture of people experiencing the healing power of Jesus and running out to tell others the Good News! Helping others and sharing what we have learned is one of the ways we help bring the Kingdom of God here to earth.

Share one way your small group has been a blessing in your life.

____

____

If you have experienced the power of the Holy Spirit through the *Unleashed* study, we ask you to consider helping others on their journey. During your quiet time this week, ask the Lord to give you the names of individuals from work, church or friends who might benefit from doing the study. Make a plan to reach out to them and see if they would consider meeting over the next 8-9 months to experience the power of connecting in small group to grow in their faith and build relationships.

Perhaps your group would like to stay together longer and continue to encourage one another as you experience life's ups and downs.

> *And let us consider how we may spur one another on toward love and good deeds, not giving up meeting together, as some are in the habit of doing, but encouraging one another—and all the more as you see the Day approaching.*
>
> Hebrews 10:24-25

Group Discussion:
Why do you think some people are in the habit of giving up meeting together?

____

____

Spend some time discussing how your group would like to connect moving forward.

____

____

Visit our website to learn more about the resources we have available for leadership development modules, discovering your identity workshop and more.

www.womeninmarketplace.net

Challenge for the week:
Pray and ask God who you might invite to participate in an *Unleashed* study.

Work

____

____

____

____

Church

____

____

____

____

Family/Friends

____

____

____

____

Who can you ask to co-facilitate with you?

____

Make a plan to reach out to the people on this list within the next two weeks. Additional tips for how to start your own small group are located on the next page.

Prayer Requests:

HOW TO START A SMALL GROUP

The following steps are provided to help you launch a *Unleashed* group. If you have questions or want to set up a call to discuss further, please contact us at info@womeninmarketplace.net.

Step 1: Find a co-facilitator

We recommend **two facilitators** for your group. Work schedules are hectic and life happens. This allows you to split the workload and keep group consistently on the schedule.

Step 2: Invite people

Ask people you know to join and invite others from their company or circle of friends who they think might be interested in attending.

Use **social media** to announce timing for information session. [If it is an open group, send your details to us at info@womeninmarketplace.net, and we will post on our FP page.]

Step 3: Information session

Prior to the start of a new group, schedule an information session to give people an opportunity to **explore** without making a commitment. Provide a way to **learn more** about what a small group is and why they should join.

Step 4: Launch:
Set up calendar meeting invite once group details are established. Order books for your group or have them order them individually prior to your first meeting.

Unleash power and purpose in your work!